The Schooner

The Schooner

Its Design and Development from 1600 to the Present

David R MacGregor

NAVAL INSTITUTE PRESS

Annapolis, Maryland

By the same author

The Tea Clippers (1952; reprinted 1972)
The China Bird (1961; enlarged and revised 1986)
Fast Sailing Ships (1973; revised edition 1988)
Square Rigged Sailing Ships (1977)
Clipper Ships (1979)
Merchant Sailing Ships 1775-1815
  (1980; enlarged and revised 1985)
Schooners in Four Centuries (1982)
The Tea Clippers 1833-1875
  (1983, enlarged and revised edition)
Merchant Sailing Ships 1815-1850 (1984)
Merchant Sailing Ships 1850-1875 (1984)
British and American Clippers (1993)

Large-scale copies of the plans reproduced here are available on application to the author at:
12 Upper Oldfield Park, Bath BA2 3JZ, England

FRONTISPIECE

One of the four-masted schooners built in Denmark was the *Richard* of 325 tons net, constructed at Svendborg of wood in 1920. Seen here in ballast, she made a fine sight with four yards on her foremast.
(F Holm-Petersen)

© 1997 by David R MacGregor

First published in Great Britain in 1997 by
Chatham Publishing, 1&2 Faulkner's Alley,
Cowcross St, London EC1M 6DD

Published and distributed in the United States of America and Canada
by the Naval Institute Press, 118 Maryland Avenue, Annapolis, Maryland 21402-5035

A Library of Congress Catalog Card No
is available on request.

ISBN 1 -55750-847-X

Manufactured in Great Britain

Contents

*Dedicated to Henrietta
and Peter Sherwin*

Introduction

OVER THE centuries there have an infinite variety of vessels in coastal waters and on the high seas, and our knowledge of them is only restricted due to the lack of methods for visually recording them in the past. But the variety of hull shapes, of rigging, of deck layouts, of colour, and of operating methods has always existed from port to port and from country to country. Schooners are certainly no exception to this and the chapter titles in this book will indicate the diversity of their activities which are world-wide. Some of these are considered 'romantic', such as privateering or smuggling illicit cargoes, whilst others are more prosaic, such as fishing or pilotage.

Superlatives often set the tone whereas the average really predominates. 'What was the biggest schooner?' is sure to be asked, and the American seven-master will probably be known, and sometimes also the existence of the American six-masters, all constructed from 1900 onwards. But who knows that the earliest vessel to be rigged as a six-masted schooner was the SS *Great Britain* built before 1850? Even before 1860 came the huge steamship *Great Eastern* with six masts, carrying gaffs on each mast and none of the masts were other than immense combinations of those to be found in topsail schooners.

This book is a greatly expanded version of the one published fifteen years ago with the title *Schooners in Four Centuries*, much of which has been re-written and new material added, both in the matter of text and also of photographs and plans. Many of the spritsail barges which were then sailing have survived as living examples of wooden trading vessels, and so too have a few ketches and schooners either as museum exhibits or in other disguises. But now the hulks which used to litter the shores and hidden creeks are mostly gone or their remains so ravaged by time or by vandals as to be scarcely recognisable.

Of the people whose assistance I acknowledged in the Introduction to the earlier edition, many are no more. But Basil Greenhill has continued as a good friend over the years and has given valuable advice on many occasions. In the matter of illustrations, David Clement has again generously made his collection freely available. Others in Great Britain who have assisted with the matter of illustrations are Mark Myers, for giving permission to use photographs taken by his father-in-law, Michael Bouquet; Janette Rosing who has aided me in collecting photographs and also loaned a print; Malcolm Darch for allowing me to use the Fairweather Collection; James Dickie for providing photographs of opium clippers from his collection; Ralph Bird for permission to use several plans he has drawn; and Brian Newbury of the Parker Gallery who has allowed me to reproduce photographs of paintings from their files. Others who have provided comments on photographs or paintings are Terry Belt and Roger Hadlee.

Several friends, recently departed, include Frode Holm-Petersen who has provided me with many photographs over forty years; Karl Kortum of the San

Francisco Maritime Museum who would frequently send over details about shipping matters; and Robert Weinstein who let me browse through his splendid collection. Others in North America to whom I am especially grateful are Captain W J Lewis Parker for providing me with illustrations to reproduce; also to Douglas Lee for data about his schooner and particularly for facts on the multi-masted schooners built in Maine, of which he has been drawing plans; likewise to Dr Charles Armour for photographs and plans of Canadian vessels.

The curators and staff at several museums have been most courteous and helpful over the years, and I am grateful for permissions to reproduce photographs in their collections; in particular I would like to thank the Peabody Museum of Salem, the Mariners Museum at Newport News, the National Maritime Museum at San Francisco; and in Great Britain the National Maritime Museum at Greenwich. Several Canadian museums have also been most helpful.

In the matter of acknowledgements, I have lost touch in several cases with persons who originally supplied illustrations, but I have continued to acknowledge the pictures to them and I apologise for having been unable to obtain their permission again. In some instances, no source was given on the photograph, and I have only been able to hint at its origin.

Of course I have been an avid collector myself for many years and always on the lookout for new illustrations. Where pictures are acknowledged to 'Author', this indicates a photograph I have taken myself; whereas 'MacGregor Collection' refers to a picture of unknown origin which I have acquired. The upheaval in moving to Bath eighteen months ago after thirty-two years at the same house in London has resulted in some documents or illustrations not having been found, which has caused difficulties in tracing owners of illustrations. However, there is more wall space here for bookshelves and paintings, thanks to my wife's indulgence and continued encouragement.

David R MacGregor
Bath, Somerset, 1997

Definitions | *1*

SMALL BOAT handling is practised by many today and gives a thrill because of the direct contact with the wind and water which can be achieved by means of a simple form of rig. A schooner is basically such a simple form, especially in the first century in which it was used, and provides an effective use of wind power as a means of propulsion, needing only a small crew to handle it. Square-rigged vessels, by contrast, require a more complicated system of rigging to control and operate the sails and thus need larger crews. Nevertheless, the three-masted square-rigged ship had been in use for some two centuries before the forerunner of the schooner appeared on the scene.

It was the square sail, lug sail and spritsail which were commonly in use in northern Europe in the sixteenth century, and it was the lug and the spritsail that could be handled by the least number of men and which performed best in working to windward. As the small-boat sailor and indeed anyone who goes afloat under sail knows only too well, it is the ability to get and keep to windward which gives safety at all times, as well as the ease of dropping and picking up moorings, of making a passage or of winning a race.

If to the lug and spritsail is added the third type, the square sail, it will be noted

In Penzance Harbour at low water, three classic forms of rig lie side-by-side. From left to right they are: a brigantine, a cutter or sloop, and a two-masted schooner (the bow of the latter having been unfortunately cut off by the photographer). The schooner is of the conventional British kind with square topsails on the foremast. The cutter sets the same form of gaff sail as found on both masts of the schooner and on the mainmast of the brigantine. (Courtesy of Frank E Gibson)

Fore side of a square topsail. Although this is of the kind to be found on a square-rigged vessel, the square sails on schooners and brigantines were similar but without so many bands of reef points.

A three-sided jib or staysail on the left and a gaff sail on the right. Although the gaff sail is secured to the mast by hoops so that it can slide up and down on the mast, there are also three ropes drawn from the leach to the gaff in order to brail the sail to the mast. For this reason, the foot of the sail is not fastened to the boom, as it will be bunched into the mast when 'brailed'. This is a quick method of furling it.

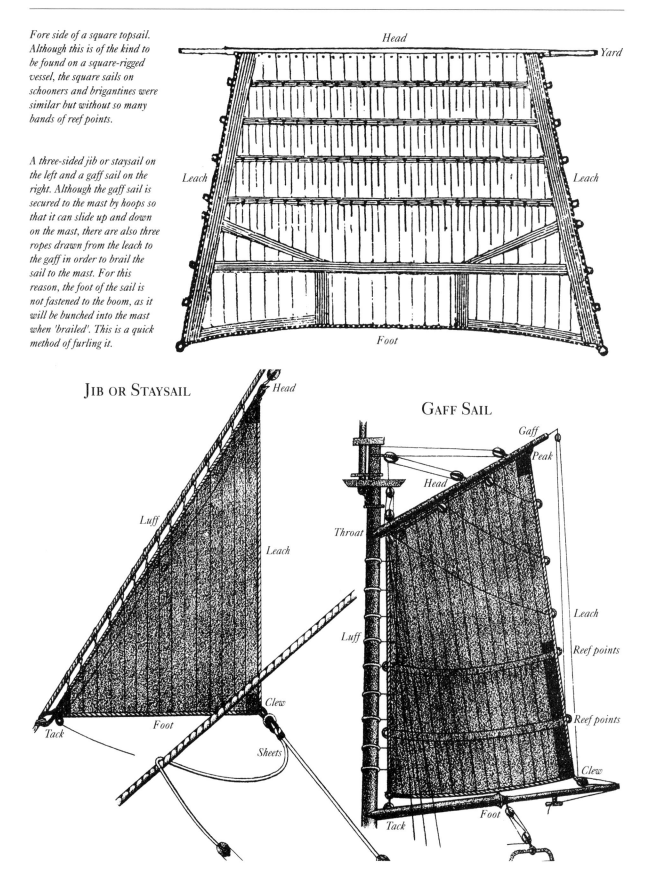

Head

Yard

Leach

Leach

Foot

JIB OR STAYSAIL

Head

Luff

Leach

Luff

Clew

Foot

Tack

Sheets

GAFF SAIL

Gaff

Peak

Head

Throat

Leach

Reef points

Reef points

Clew

Tack

Foot

that all three types are four-sided: the upper edge of the square sail and lug are fastened to a spar called a 'yard', the vertical edges or 'leeches' are loose, and the lower edge or 'foot' may likewise be loose or fixed to a spar; the spritsail – as its name implies – has a spar called a 'sprit' to hold up its peak, or uppermost corner, and one of its vertical edges is secured to the mast.

The gaff sail, which is the principal form of canvas in a schooner, is different again: it has the shape of the spritsail with the sprit omitted but with a spar called a 'gaff' supporting the 'head' or upper edge of the sail, and the inner end of the gaff pivoting on the mast. One vertical edge or 'luff' is secured to the mast, and there is often a spar or 'boom' along the foot of the sail. Accompanying illustrations indicate some of these points.

In *Man on the Ocean* (1874), R M Ballantyne describes 'The Schooner' in these words:

This is the most elegant and, for small craft, the most manageable vessel that floats. Its proportions are more agreeable to the eye than those of any other species of craft, and its rig is in favour with owners of yachts – especially with those whose yachts are large. The schooner's distinctive peculiarities are, that it carries two masts, which usually 'rake aft' or lean back a good deal; and its rig is chiefly fore-

Another important rig is that of the brig which has only two masts, square-rigged on each. In this unidentified vessel, the masts have been shortened so that no royal yards are crossed. On the mainmast, the head of the spanker is held to the mast by hoops that slide on the gaff which permits the sail to be gathered into the mast without lowering the gaff. Actually this vessel is really a 'snow' as the spanker is not set on a boom. (MacGregor Collection)

and-aft, like the sloop. Of the two masts, the *after* one is the *main-mast*. The other is termed the *fore-mast*. The sails of a schooner are – the *main-sail* and *gaff* [*topsail*] on the *main-mast*; the *fore-sail*, *fore-top-sail*, and *fore-top-gallant-sail* (the last two being square sails), on the fore-mast. In front of the fore-mast are the *stay-sail*, the *jib*, and the *flying-jib*; these last are triangular sails . . . Schooners sometimes carry a large square-sail, which is spread when the wind is 'dead aft'. They are much used in the coasting trade; and one of their great advantages is that they can be worked with fewer 'hands' than sloops of the same size.

Of course, schooners can have more than two masts but the sails carried should be principally fore-and-aft ones, although numerous variations will be shown in the illustrations assembled here, with staysails and Bermudian sails replacing gaff sails. The same sort of gaff sails given to schooners can also be found on the sloop, cutter, ketch, brigantine and barquentine. Some ketches were larger than schooners and proved a more economical form of rig. 'Leg-of-mutton' or Bermudian sails were rare on trading schooners except on the aftermost mast of American Pacific Coast vessels.

Schooners were used mainly for pleasure in their earliest forms but since 1700 have carried every conceivable cargo: they have been employed in estuaries, coastal work and ocean voyages; they have been humble carriers or smart clippers, privateers or slavers, fishermen, pilot boats, or school ships. Examples of most types are given here. However, there is insufficient space to explore too deeply into any single vessel, and so this will be a broad and general survey.

Another form of fore-and-aft rig was the ketch, as seen in this view of the Mount Carmel *of Scilly, of 54 tons built in 1892. The mizen mast is shorter than the mainmast but carries a similar form of gaff sail and there is no topsail; a few ketches carried a single yard on the mainmast to set a big square sail. A ketch would probably carry one less hand than a schooner.* (H Oliver Hill)

Two-Masted Boats 2

ALTHOUGH THE word 'schooner' is attributed first to a chance remark made by a spectator at the launch of a two-masted vessel in New England in about 1713, other craft with similar arrangements of fore-and-aft sails had existed in various forms for over a century. The earliest known illustration appears to be an ink drawing by the Dutch artist Rool, dated 1600, in which the Burgomasters of Amsterdam are disporting themselves on their yacht, which is running before the wind goose-winged, with her sails boomed out on opposite sides. There is a 'leg-of-mutton' sail with a very short gaff set on each mast; the mainsail on the taller mast is much larger than the foresail, and the foremast is stepped right up in the eyes of the boat; there is no bowsprit and no staysail or jib. The leeboard on the port side is drawn hauled up, and the sheer of the hull sweeps up to a high stern. This illustration is reproduced in Arthur H Clark's *History of Yachting 1600-1815* (1904).

In the same book, Clark has an engraving of a dozen or so such craft greeting Queen Mary of France at Amsterdam in 1638 and each firing a bow gun in salute. Other similar illustrations exist, including Hartgers' view of New Amsterdam – as New York was then known – drawn in about 1627, and a painting by Adam Willaerts of Batavia harbour in 1649. In his book, *Sloops & Shallops*, William A Baker writes

A Dutch speeljaght *painted by Simon de Vlieger (1600-53) with short gaffs and high ornamented stern. There are no shrouds and the leeboard is hauled up.* (Courtesy of the Rupert Preston Gallery)

The mezzotint referred to in the text as published in The Mariner's Mirror *(Vol I) was possibly made from this painting, attributed to Van de Velde the younger. At least they are broadly similar, but this illustration shows the rigging, sails, flags and hulls quite clearly and distinctly. Two schooners are here, each with a headsail on a bowsprit, and that in the foreground has a broadside of six guns. On the left is a typical cutter with an elaborately carved stern and her mainsail brailed in.* (Courtesy of the Parker Gallery)

that there is evidence that such vessels carried a bowsprit and a triangular headsail by about 1650.

The Dutch employed the word *jaght* to define a craft built to sail swiftly and of light construction, whether it was for merchant or naval purposes. Their Admiralty yachts and their State yachts, which acted in the same way as Revenue cutters did in England, carried a single gaff sail or spritsail, together with a bowsprit supporting two headsails, and there was sometimes a square topsail. Some hulls went up to 70ft in length. In England, the word 'yacht' was corrupted to mean any craft used for pleasure. The Dutch used the term *speeljaght* for a pleasure craft and these were generally two-masted and of the kind already described with their 'leg-of-mutton' sails. Illustrations depict them in harbours or estuaries, and so they were probably not more than about 35ft in length.

In the seventeenth century, two-masted boats of this kind would have been classed as 'sloops' from the Dutch word *sloepe*. Thomas Blanckley's celebrated definition of this word in his *Naval Expositor*, compiled in 1732, describes sloops with one, two or three masts, having square or round sterns, and capable of setting Bermudian, 'leg-of-mutton', square, lug or smack sails. The last-named probably refers to a gaff sail rather than a spritsail.

By 1700 there appears to have been little change in the two-masted rig, although the bowsprit and jib were now established, and craft of larger size were obviously being constructed. Arthur H Clark, in his book on 'Yachting', quotes from a marine dictionary published at Amsterdam in 1702 which lists dimensions of a two-masted 'sloop' with the following measurements. Hull: length 42ft, breadth 9ft, stem 5.5ft high, sternpost 7ft high and raked 2ft aft. Masts and spars: foremast 15ft, fore gaff

10ft, fore boom 11.5ft, mainmast 24ft, main gaff 12.5ft, main boom 21ft.

One of these two-masted 'sloops' is illustrated in *The Mariner's Mirror* (Vol I), being taken from an undated Van de Velde painting, but it must be prior to 1707 when the younger artist of that name died. The vessel is flying British colours and has a broadside of five guns. The mainsail is much larger than the foresail and there is a bowsprit and headsail.

Therefore the rig was obviously being copied and used in England which was only natural, considering the close trade links and proximity of the two coastlines. A large example was the *Royal Transport* of 220 tons, carrying 20 guns and a crew of 100 men, which was launched at Chatham in 1695 and given by William III to Peter the Great two years later.

An interesting survival of the seventeenth-century rig of the two-masted boat without a headsail may be found in the Block Island boats as recounted by E P Morris in *The Fore-and-Aft Rig in America*. There were sixty such craft in 1883 but they had all vanished by 1925 with the exception of a full-size replica. They were double-ended craft intended to be launched from a beach, yet they had a 'V' bottom; and length varied from 18 to 26ft. Incidentally, Block Island lies off the coast of Rhode Island.

Of course, during the seventeenth century a more common form of the two-masted rig, to judge by surviving paintings, was the square-rigged ketch with yards on both masts, and a number of them were in use in England; there was also the brigantine.

A coastal scene with a sprit-rigged Dutch boat on the left, a schooner in the foreground and a ship in the distance at anchor. The schooner has boomless sails with short gaffs, and the projecting beakhead permits a forestay to be rigged. (National Maritime Museum, London)

3 | *Colonial America*

TWO-MASTED vessels rigged with lateen yards on each mast are portrayed in panoramic views of New York harbour in the second half of the seventeenth century, but after the year 1700 the lateen only appears as a mizen, it having been superseded by the gaff. This applies to views of both New York and New England. As regards illustrations of the gaff rig, William Burgis' view of New York (1717) has many three-masted square-rigged ships and also numerous single-masted craft with gaff sails, but apparently no fore-and-aft two-masters. None of the cutters appears to carry a square topsail, not even the largest which mounts a broadside of five guns, and some of them have quite short gaffs. There is one two-master rigged down to the lower masts which are of equal height and with her yards lowered on the lifts; there is also the mastless hulk of a two-master with a tall flagpole set up amidships.

However, in his 1725 view of Boston, William Burgis has drawn a much greater variety of craft. In addition to the many three-masted square-rigged ships, there are two brigantines in the modern sense of the word, with two square sails on the foremast and a large gaff mainsail; there is a ketch, square-rigged on the mainmast and with a lateen on the mizen; there are many single-masted craft, of which certainly two carry two yards on a tall mast; and there are also four two-masters, two of which

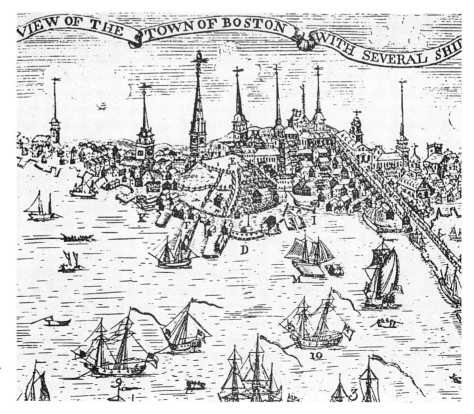

Six years after Paul Revere made an engraving of British troops landing in Boston, he produced another one showing a wider panorama of the town and harbour of which this is a detail. Some of the warships are still swinging to their anchors in the same positions but there are more small craft. These latter comprise two schooners at anchor with two yards on each mast; a fore-and-aft schooner under sail and another at anchor; there are also several two-masted boats without bowsprits. This is a modern reproduction of the old engraving. (MacGregor Collection)

16

A Dutch schooner and a British cutter at Curaçao in 1786. The Mariners' Museum has a painting done a year earlier showing an almost identical schooner at this port, but flying British colours. The schooner here has a ringtail boom rigged out but she crosses no yards. (Courtesy of the Parker Gallery)

are undoubtedly gaff-rigged on each mast. One of the latter is under sail with a single headsail, whilst the other at anchor has two stays from foremast to bowsprit, the gaff sails being triced up with the clew hauled out to the boom end.

It was in the seaport of Gloucester, Massachusetts, that the story originated of who first invented the schooner. According to tradition it occurred about 1713 when Andrew Robinson was launching a new vessel and upon her entering the water, a spectator called out, 'Oh, how she scoons!', whereupon Robinson is said to have remarked: 'A scooner let her be'.

Writing in 1904, Arthur H Clark stated that no marine use of the word 'scooner' had been found prior to 1713, and he cited the derivation of the word from the Dutch 'schoon', taken from a Dutch-Latin dictionary published in 1599, meaning 'beautiful, fair, lovely'. He added that in thirteen applications given in the dictionary for the use of the word, not one had a nautical connotation. Just as in the case

Model of HMS Sultana *made
from Howard Chapelle's plans
with yards for a square topsail
only on the foremast, although
the log-book infers that there
were topsails on each mast.*
(Courtesy of Model Expo
Inc, Mt Pocono,
Pennsylvania)

of coining the word 'clipper' for a fast-sailing ship, its use having been generally applied to horses, so 'scoons' need have had no maritime background. Writing in 1927, E P Morris concluded that the story was 'nothing more than a picturesque adornment of the Gloucester tradition'.

In any case, there is sufficient evidence to prove that vessels of this rig had already existed for at least one hundred years on both sides of the Atlantic, such as those described in Chapter 2. In America it is thought that some of the fishing

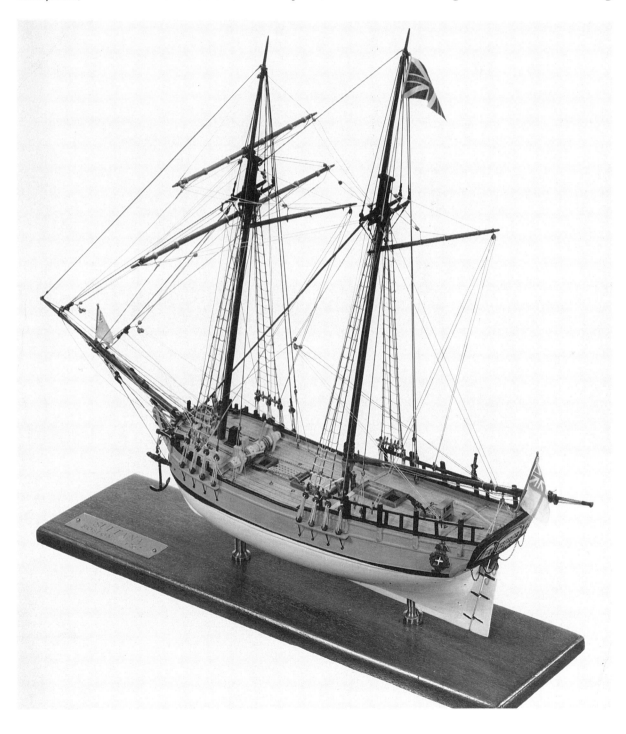

Model of HMS Sultana *made from Howard Chapelle's plans with yards for a square topsail only on the foremast, although the log-book infers that there were topsails on each mast.* (Courtesy of Model Expo Inc, Mt Pocono, Pennsylvania)

ketches might have been rigged in a similar fashion, which would have been an improvement on the earlier rig of a single sail on each mast. It is contrary to tradition to imagine that a new class of vessel, termed a 'scooner', suddenly made its appearance and was at once universally adopted. The 'scooning' of the Gloucester two-master may have applied to a new hull-form rather than any alteration of an established rig.

However, it is only sensible to employ the commonly-accepted spelling of 'schooner' to describe vessels of this rig, although the English continued to call a large decked schooner a 'sloop' as late as about 1750, and a small open one a 'shallop'. The idiosyncrasies of registration officials and of shipbuilders over rig nomenclature have greatly confused rig evolution for the modern student and possibly curtailed the acknowledgement of the introduction of new and varied types of rig.

Today we are always trying to pin names on things and historians often regret the anonymity adopted in past centuries, so that to find a named schooner of large size that was afloat in 1736 is something worth noting. She was the *St Ann* and it was in that year that this fine-lined Portuguese dispatch schooner reached Portsmouth, where a surveyor of the Royal Navy took off her lines. His plan was acquired by the Swedish naval architect, Chapman, on a visit to England, and therefore the plan resides in a Stockholm museum. She was reported as having been built in America and sold to Portugal. Howard I Chapelle redrew the lines plan and reconstructed a sail plan from the listed spar dimensions, and these plans are reproduced in his book *Search for Speed under Sail*. The *St Ann* had a narrow, fine-lined hull with hollow floors and large deadrise; she had dimensions of 58ft 2in (length at the rail), 11ft 10in (moulded breadth), 6ft 10in (keel rabbet to deck) and 36.5 tons. She had fairly short gaffs with three yards on the foremast. It is interesting that the topgallant yard was termed a 'pidgeon' yard. The French also called the topgallant yard after a bird, in this case a parrot, using the word *perroquet*.

As trade with the West Indies was increasing, schooners were becoming larger in size, and in particular the proportions of the gaff sails were altering as the gaffs were made longer. Economy in manpower was the keynote which was why the sloop with a big single gaff sail and two or three square sails was gradually being replaced by the schooner, with its smaller sail units. Schooners were also popular in the rapidly-expanding fishing industry: in 1721 there were 120 of them at Marblehead averaging 50 tons in size; twenty years later the number of boats had increased to 160. Owing to the activities of numerous pirates and little in the way of naval protection, schooners were often designed to sail fast, and some were armed.

In the thirty or so years prior to the War of Independence, Marblehead schooners gained a reputation for speed and the Royal Navy purchased six of them in the years 1767-68. One was the *Sultana*, built at Boston in 1767 and bought the following year. She was of 50.65 tons with a length on deck of 50ft 6in and a breadth of 16ft 1in. She had steepish deadrise with rounded bilges and hollows in the lower port of her entrance and run. Another schooner, the *Chaleur*, was somewhat larger at 121 tons with a plain, unadorned stem. She could set square topsails on both masts, an arrangement that was becoming increasingly popular on both sides of the Atlantic up to 1815 or so. Often topgallants could, in addition, be set on each mast above the topsails, with studdingsails as well. Plans of these schooners and others built in America for the Royal Navy are preserved in the British Admiralty records held by the National Maritime Museum.

In *The National Watercraft Collection*, which describes the collection of models at the Smithsonian Institution, Howard Chapelle quotes from the Boston *Gazette* of May 1761 which warned of a 12-gun French privateer off the coast which had originally been a 'Marblehead fisherman', and now had black upperworks on one side of her hull but was painted yellow with white strakes on the other side. In 1777, the same paper warned of another Marblehead-built schooner, her bottom painted white and of about 70 tons with a crew of forty men. Her rig is described as having a 'lug foresail and two standing topsails'. The topsails would be a square topsail on each topmast and the mainsail, although not mentioned, would have been a gaff sail. Lug foresails were occasionally to be seen, and even persisted into the nineteenth century.

A painting in the Peabody Museum of the schooner *Baltick*, dated 1765, is constantly being reproduced, probably because it is considered to be the earliest known portrait of a named schooner. Her foremast is stepped well forward, there is a high steeved bowsprit, a square topsail and big square foresail in addition to the gaff sail on each mast. Steering on all schooners at this date was by means of a tiller, and all these schooners had square sterns.

Lines plan of the armed schooner Sultana *after being taken into the Royal Navy in 1768. With a broad hull, steep deadrise and fine lines she must have been a speedy craft. This plan was drawn by Howard I Chapelle from a draught in the Admiralty archives.* (Courtesy of Model Expo Inc, Mt Pocono, Pennsylvania)

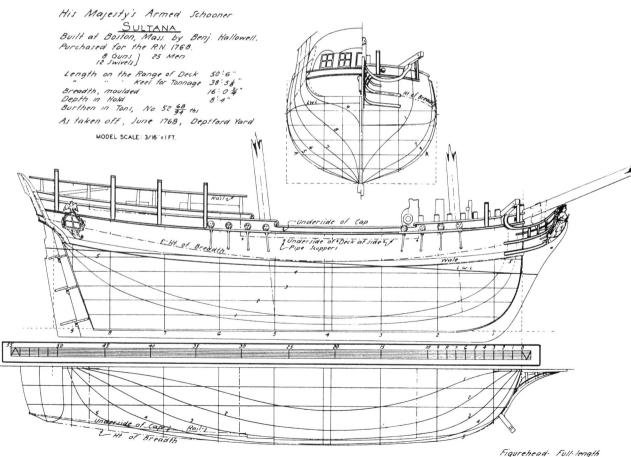

His Majesty's Armed Schooner
SULTANA
Built at Boston, Mass. by Benj. Hallowell.
Purchased for the R.N. 1768.
8 Guns } 25 Men
12 Swivels }
Length on the Range of Deck   50'6"
  "   "   Keel for Tonnage   38'5⅝"
Breadth, moulded   16'0¾"
Depth in Hold   8'4"
Burthen in Tons, No 52 68/94 ths
As taken off, June 1768, Deptford Yard
MODEL SCALE: 3/16"=1 FT.

Lines shown to inside of plank.

Figurehead- Full-length Woman, — removed by Royal Navy

Shallops and Chebacco Boats | *4*

TWO TYPES of schooner-rigged craft had emerged in America by 1750: one was the ocean-going schooner used on long coastal voyages or in the deep sea fisheries, and rigged with square as well as fore-and-aft canvas; the other was a generally smaller craft used for estuary and inshore work, but noteworthy because she only carried two gaff sails of approximately similar size, without either bowsprit or jib. Of this latter category were the shallops which were decked vessels rigged with gaff sails or spritsails, and with the foremast stepped right up in the eyes of the boat.

Such craft were also in use in England and there is an interesting painting at the National Maritime Museum by John Clevely, which depicts various vessels on the River Stour near Ipswich, including two shallops. What makes this picture unique is that an X-ray photograph of the shallops reveals that their rig was originally that of a gaff sail on each mast, with a short gaff, but that this had been over-painted, thereby altering the rig to that of two spritsails. English shallops were commonly

Ink drawing attributed to Samuel Owen (1768-1857) of a shallop hoisting sail. Two of the crew are inked in and there is a third drawn in pencil or he may be an alternate for the one hoisting the mainsail. The pencil drawings at the top of the sheet appear to be unconnected with the shallop. (MacGregor Collection)

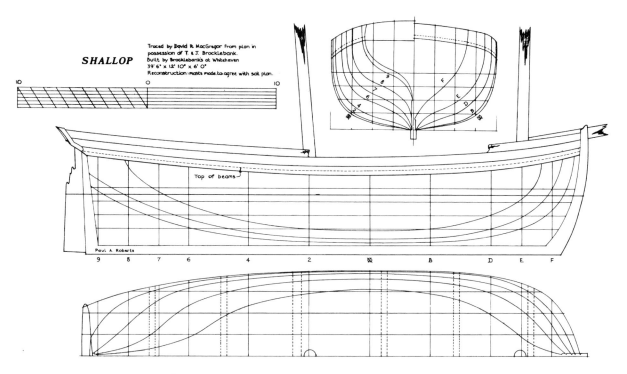

SHALLOP

Traced by David R. MacGregor from plan in possession of T. & J. Brocklebank.
Built by Brocklebank's at Whitehaven
39' 6" x 12' 10" x 6' 0"
Reconstruction: masts made to agree with sail plan.

Top of beams

Paul A. Roberts

Above: Lines plan of unnamed shallop built in 1806 at Whitehaven by Brocklebank with a capacity of twenty-one hogsheads. Plan traced by the author from original and re-drawn in ink by Paul Roberts. She had a reputation of sailing fast. The dotted lines presumably indicate deck beams.

Below: Sail plan of Brocklebank's shallop of 1806 based on a tracing of the original made by the author.

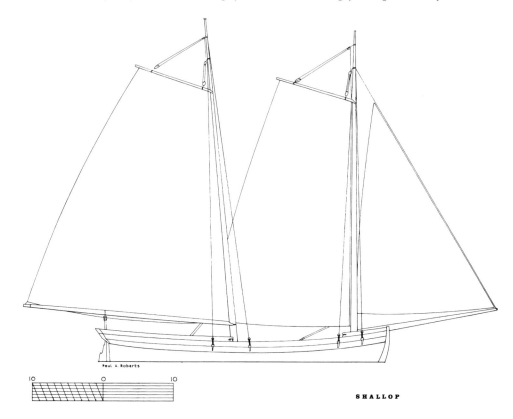

Paul A. Roberts

SHALLOP

smaller than American ones and were often un-decked. An engraving by Kips of the River Thames at Lambeth, dated *c*1671, depicts just a craft measuring about 25ft in length. Another important difference between American and English shallops was that the latter usually carried a bowsprit from which a large jib was set.

An example can be had in one of the four shallops built by Daniel Brocklebank between 1799 and 1806 of which there is a lines plan and a sail plan. This was the largest of the four with dimensions of 39ft 6in (length overall), 12ft 10in (breadth moulded) and 6ft 0in (depth of hold). From gunwale to hounds, the foremast measured 36ft 0in and the mainmast 38ft 6in; the length of the bowsprit outside the stem was 15ft 0.5in and each gaff was 11ft 0in. No dimension was given for the main boom.

This particular shallop was unnamed but a note on the lines plan states: 'Much approved of being of an Easy Draught of Water and Sailing Fast'. She could carry twenty-one hogsheads. She is a broad vessel with short, sharp ends that have marked hollows in the lower waterlines; the cross-sections are very rounded up to the load line. The lines plan was drawn at a scale of ½in to 1ft and a sail plan on the reverse at half scale is assumed to be of the same vessel. It is a very simple sail plan with pole masts and the minimum of rigging; there are only two shrouds to each

Copied from a photograph taken by Calvert Jones in Swansea in the 1840s showing two of the 21ft schooner-rigged pilot boats. The bowsprits have been run in-board. Larger decked boats were introduced c1860.

mast and a single fore stay; the peak and throat halliards have a single tackle in each case. No reef points are drawn on the original nor any sheets, so the latter have been reconstructed. Brocklebank's craft has six deck beams, indicated by dotted lines on the plan.

After the end of the American War of Independence, there was a shortage of the larger schooners for the growing coastal fisheries of New England, and shallops of similar size to Brocklebank's became popular. In *Sloops & Shallops* (1966), William A Baker describes how the naming of certain local fishing boats was derived from Chebacco parish in the town of Ipswich, Massachusetts. The Chebacco boats at the close of the eighteenth century averaged 38ft long and 11ft wide; the hull was basically double-ended with the wales taken round to the sternpost rather than to where the wing transom and quarter piece met, as in a square stern. The after deck and the bulwarks were continued to provide a short overhang abaft the sternpost. A smaller version with a square stern was the 'dogbody'. The Chebacco boats were built in New England, New Brunswick and Nova Scotia, and from them in the nineteenth century were developed the larger Saint John 'woodboats'.

In this view of Padstow Harbour, two small schooner-rigged barges can be observed with their gaff sails hoisted; there was a staysail set from the foremast. The hatchway occupied the space between the masts and there was little freeboard when they were full of cargo. Copied from an old postcard.

A surviving example of a shallop in the British Isles is the *Peggy*, built in 1791, at Castletown, Isle of Man, where she is still preserved. She was measured in 1968 by D K Jones and W Clarke. She is clinker-built with marked hollows in her garboards; she has more deadrise than Brocklebank's shallop and finer, convex ends; she has a square tuck stern. The sail plan is similar to the Brocklebank vessels. As originally built, the *Peggy* had two drop keels.

Various examples of two-masted boats are to be found in other places. For instance, open-decked, schooner-rigged lighters or shallops were to be seen in Padstow harbour, deeply laden with cargo, in the first decade of the twentieth century.

Privateers and Baltimore Clippers | 5

SOME OF the fast-sailing schooners built in Massachusetts were described in Chapter 3, but there were two other important types. One was the 'Virginia pilot boat' with her flush deck, deep drag aft, practically no bulwarks and only primitive accommodation. They were rigged with two well-raked pole masts which carried a gaff mainsail on a boom, a gaff foresail without a boom and a jib set on a bowsprit; square canvas was rare, but there was usually a large main topmast staysail. Such craft were also popular at New York and on the Delaware, and averaged 35 to 45ft in length.

The other type was built on Chesapeake Bay and was a bigger schooner altogether, carrying a square topsail and topgallant on the foremast which was often repeated on the mainmast. Like the Virginia type, there was a low profile hull with a deep drag aft, combined with steep deadrise and fine waterlines to give maximum speed under sail. Even by 1757 some of these schooners were 80ft in length and mounted fourteen guns. This was the type which became known as a 'Baltimore clipper'. Surveyors to the Royal Navy often took lines off captured schooners, drew up their plans, added some deck details and tabulated the lengths of their masts and spars on the plan. They rarely drew out the sail plans, although a notable exception is that of the three-masted schooner *Revenge*, built at Baltimore in 1805 and taken into the Royal Navy under the name of *Flying Fish*. The preservation of such plans amongst the Admiralty collection of draughts enables one to obtain a good idea of the splendid schooners sailing the high seas in those days and to estab-

The Challenge *exhibits the limit of square canvas that could be set on a schooner. Here the yards on the main are shorter than those on the fore, and the square sail from the fore yard has been clewed up.* (Courtesy of the Peabody Museum of Salem)

Lines plan, deck layout and sail plan of the Virginia pilot boat Katy *(c1800). Her dimensions were 56ft length, 15ft 3in breadth and 52 tons. Plan drawn by M A Edson jnr. (Courtesy of Model Expo Inc, Mt Pocono, Pennsylvania)*

lish the fact that the design was truly American and not taken from French luggers, which is the popular legend.

An example of a typical Virginia pilot boat can be found in a reconstruction made by M A Edson Jnr using the lines plan in plate XXV from Steel's *Naval Architecture*, first published in 1805. Dimensions on this plan are 56ft 0in (length on deck), 15ft 3in (extreme breadth) and 52 tons. There is a fair amount of deadrise with hollow garboards and rounded bilges; the entrance is convex but the run has some hollow up to the load line; there is appreciable drag aft, with a raking sternpost and a

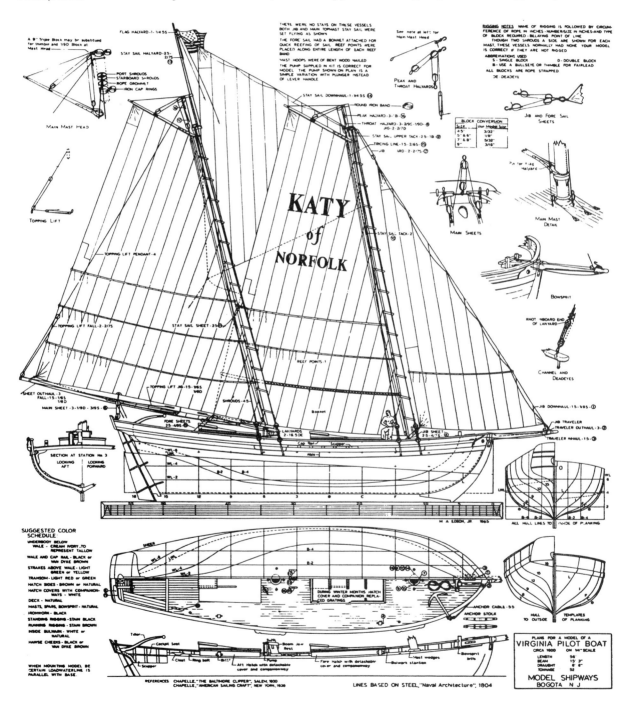

An unidentified schooner photographed in stereo at Havana. Judging by the size of the persons aboard her, she is not a large craft, and she appears to be a survivor from the past with her low-peaked main gaff and boomless foresail; the topmasts are rather short and there is a yard on the foremast. (Courtesy of the National Maritime Museum, San Francisco)

square tuck stern. This description applies equally well to Edson's reconstruction which he has called *Katy* of Norfolk, Virginia. No spar dimensions are given for this 52-ton schooner in Steel's Art of *Making Masts, Yards . . .* (2nd ed 1816 8vo). The only schooner for which spars are given is a vessel of 110 tons with topsail and topgallant yards on each mast, and there is neither a lines plan nor an offset table referring to it. This reconstructed plan uses material in books by Howard I Chapelle, and the spar dimensions and deck layout were evidently derived from such sources.

In his *Search for Speed under Sail*, Chapelle gives the lines and sail plan of the small pilot boat *Swift* of Norfolk, Virginia, which sailed across the Atlantic to Cork in 1794. Her general appearance is somewhat like the reconstructed *Katy*, although the latter is drawn as 7ft longer. The Admiralty, on more than one occasion, ordered copies of these small pilot-boat schooners to be built both in Bermuda and in the United Kingdom.

David Steel reproduced lines plans of two other Virginia schooners: on plate XXIII there is a plan of 'A Virginia Built Boat Fitted for a Privateer' with a length of 81ft 4in and of 158 tons; plate XXIV contains the lines plan of 'A Fast Sailing Schooner' with a length of 62ft and 83 tons. Unlike the other two vessels, the latter has an old-fashioned head with space for a figurehead. Steel never gives a proper description of the schooners, and his comments are confined to the following:

The Virginian, Bermudian, and other smaller vessels, of that description, have all been selected from such whose delicacy of form under water was found to give them the excellencies required in vessels for fast sailing. They are recommended, upon the honour of the authors, as vessels that have actually been built, and that have proved the truth of these assertions beyond dispute.

Right: Sail and rigging plan of
HMS Sea Lark, *ex-*Fly, *drawn
by Paul Roberts. It was
reconstructed from spar
dimensions listed on the
original lines plan and also
from a reconstructed sail plan
of the schooner kindly supplied
by Howard I Chapelle.*

Below: Lines plan of HMS Sea
Lark, *ex-*Fly, *redrawn by
Paul Roberts from Admiralty
draughts in the National
Maritime Museum, London.
Reconstruction: particulars
taken from various draughts
for the longitudinal section and
deck details.*

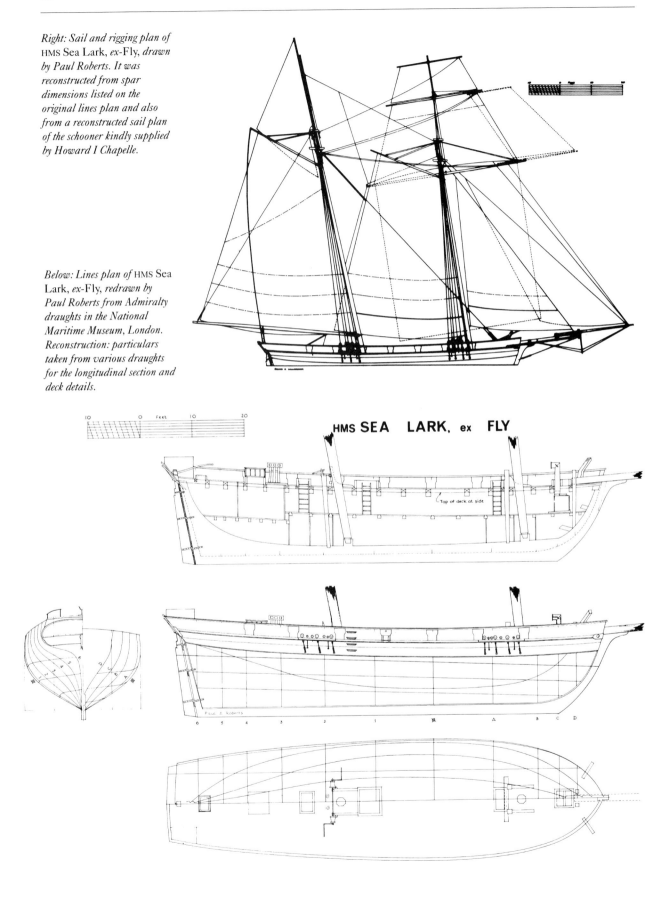

HMS SEA LARK, ex FLY

Naval architecture in the principal maritime nations of Europe had developed over the years along established lines, but in the newly-developed American States ship design was not only experimental but was made to suit the circumstances of the moment. Ornamentation was virtually non-existent and the stem rarely had anything more than a fiddle head under the bowsprit, which provided the latter with additional support in the form of a knee to which the gammon lashing could be secured. The bulwarks were only high enough to allow gun ports to be formed in them. An example of an extremely fine-lined schooner was the *Lynx*, built at Baltimore in 1812 and captured the following year, when she was taken into the Royal Navy under the name of *Musquidobit*. She measured 94ft 7in length on deck, 24ft 0in extreme breadth, 10ft 3in depth in hold and 223 tons. She had great deadrise with long, sharp lines.

Between 1783 when the War of Independence terminated and 1812 when the Naval War began, it was found that Baltimore clippers built on extreme lines did not carry enough cargo and so the hull-form was made somewhat fuller. Nevertheless, they remained fast and fine-lined by most standards. An example of this modified class was the *Fly* which was captured in 1811 some 50 miles off the Scilly Islands and taken into the Royal Navy in the following year under the name of *Sea Lark*.

Dimensions given on the plan of HMS *Sea Lark* are 81ft 3in length on deck, 22ft 8in extreme breadth, 9ft 10in depth of hold and 178 tons. Her hull-form has fine, convex waterlines, with hardly any concavity in the run, a sternpost that possesses less rake than some schooners, steep deadrise with rounded bilges and little tumblehome. Deck fittings are shown on both plan and longitudinal section, and have been combined here on a single drawing from two Admiralty draughts. She has no windlass but there are riding bitts abaft the foremast and a capstan abaft the mainmast. The longitudinal section shows the arrangement fitted by the Royal Navy. The sail and rigging plan opposite has been reconstructed from the spar dimensions listed on her draught and also from a reconstruction kindly furnished me by Howard Chapelle, which has been followed for the rigging and sails. The great height of the lower masts and the large hoist given to the gaff sails were prominent features of the Baltimore clipper schooners and provide a striking contrast to sail plans of British vessels. The American schooner often sheeted the square sail set from her fore lower yard to a boom, which together with a square topsail and topgallant gave an immense amount of square canvas when running before the wind. Had it not been for the sketch of the *Midas* (page 32), such an assortment of flying kites would not have been contemplated.

The existence of several three-masted schooners was reported during the second half of the eighteenth century and the earliest actual illustration refers to one captured in 1806. This was the *Revenge* which was built at Baltimore in 1805 and captured the following year; when taken into the Royal Navy her name was altered to *Flying Fish*. She could carry ten 9pdr guns or 12pdr carronades. In 1808 she measured 78ft 8in (length on range of deck), 21ft 7in (breadth extreme), 7ft 10in (depth in hold) and 150 tons. She had steep deadrise with straight floors and the maximum beam was at the top of the bulwarks. She was described as well-built and a fast sailer, but to safely carry such a large area of canvas she was heavily ballasted with pig iron, and constructed of light timber such as cedar. There were square topsails on fore and main and, in addition, a tiny fore topgallant; the mizen was much shorter, the truck of the topmast being below the head of the main lower mast. Studding sails were rigged out and there was a ringtail to the mizen gaff sail. Six three-masted schooners were ordered to be built at Bermuda in 1807, using her plans.

During the Naval War of 1812, the size of Chesapeake schooners increased to 115ft long on deck and this was found to be about the maximum size that could be handled safely; even then, it resulted in the main boom becoming an unwieldy spar. After the end of this war, brigs and brigantines were increasingly employed on ocean trades, and the construction of sharp-bodied schooners was largely for sale to owners in Central and South America who used them as privateers, warships or for the carriage of illicit cargoes. Not a few were also employed to carry slaves.

An account of a voyage in a Baltimore clipper was published in 1847 as one of the chapters in *Life on the Ocean*. Its author, George Little, born in 1792, had a poetic turn of phrase. Unfortunately he omits to give the schooner's name:

This rakish three-masted schooner is of the type used for privateering between 1790 and 1815. Small square topsails were carried on fore and main above the long lower masts, and the mizen is given an absurd rake aft. (Lithograph by J Rogers dated 1820)

Once more then [in December 1825], I am in command of one of the most beautiful models of a vessel that ever floated on the ocean – I mean a Baltimore clipper schooner, of one hundred and forty tons burthen, with proportions scrupulously exact as if turned out of a mould. The workmanship was in all respects as neatly executed as if intended as a beautiful specimen of cabinet excellence; her spars were in perfect symmetry of proportions with the hull, and she sat upon the water like the seabird that sleeps at ease on the mountain billow. The destination of this beautiful craft was a hazardous one, because it was in the vicinity of those seas infested by pirates, viz. the Gulf of Mexico. Her intended employment was main-

ly to bring specie from thence to the United States. She was well armed and manned, and possessed a pair of heels, as report had it, that would outstrip the wind.

The crew numbered sixteen, and on this passage she passed the Moro light on the seventh night after leaving Cape Henry, out of Baltimore. At Tampico, Campeachy and other ports, specie, indigo, cochineal and logwood were loaded for Baltimore, and the return passage was made to complete a round voyage of seven weeks. George Little made six such voyages in command, and gives a graphic description of a brush with a pirate. He was awakened from sleep by the mate, sometime after midnight, to be told that there was a vessel close astern within musket shot. The schooner's escape occurred during the night, but there must have been some light for the vessels to be able to see each other:

The schooner was at this time running under foresail alone, the other sails being lowered down, but not furled . . . The stranger rounded to under our lee, and presented one of the most frightful specimens of a piratical craft that I had ever witnessed. He hailed in broken English, ordered me to heave to, and he would send a boat on board. Perceiving at once that the commander was either no sailor, or that he had mistaken the character of my vessel by running his craft to leeward, I took advantage of his ignorance. My men were stationed, some at the main-halyards, others at the fore-topsail and jib-halyards, and as soon as his boat was swinging in the tackles over the side, they had orders to hoist the sails with all possible despatch, and at the same time the most profound silence was to be observed. I knew this was our only chance, to make the best of our way, and then run the hazard of her fire: for if the pirate's boat was permitted to come on board, all would then be lost. Therefore I preferred the chance of having some of our spars cut away, or even the loss of some of our lives, than to give up the vessel with the absolute certainty that the whole of us would be sacrificed by these atrocious marauders.

At length the looked for moment came, the pirate's boat was swung in tackles over the side, our sails went cheerily aloft, and in a few moments our craft was bounding over the sea at the rate of ten knots per hour. Quickly there was a broad sheet of flame issuing from the pirate's bows, and whistling came the deadly shot, which fell at least a quarter of a mile ahead of us. My lads were all firm and undaunted. It was a moment that called for energy and decision of character. Shot after shot passed over us, but as yet none had done any execution, and as it became necessary to increase our speed, in order to get out of gun-shot if possible, orders were given to get the squaresail aloft, ease off the main-sheet, and run the long nine-pounder aft. These orders were instantly executed, and with the additional press of canvass, she, like a dolphin when hard chased by the ravenous shark, seemed to jump out of the water, for she was now running twelve knots, and the pirate as the shark, sped on in full chase, under a cloud of sail, keeping up the while a brisk fire with single shot; but as the distance between us was increasing every moment, and the pirate, no doubt becoming exasperated at our superior sailing, yawed and gave us his whole broadside, which cut away the lower studding-

In this watercolour sketch by Admiral Philip Brown, entitled 'The Midas *of Baltimore bound to Bordeaux', the schooner is drawn stern-on with the masts in line, so that the gaff sail on the foremast is hidden by that on the main, and the square sails are those set from the foremast. She has a great variety of flying kites set: a ringtail; two watersails – one below the gaff sail and the other below the square sail; the clew of the latter hauled out on a passaree boom and the head extended by a short head stick at the outer end.* (MacGregor Collection)

sail boom, and one shot passed through our squaresail. This was his last success, for by the time he hauled up again in our wake and fired the next shot, it fell short of the mark. Then we returned his coaxing civilities in compliments of his own heart's choice, by letting him have a shot from our long nine-pounder . . . In fifteen minutes from this time we were far beyond the reach of his shot, and continued to run under a press of canvass during the remainder of the night. The next morning, our unwelcome companion, the pirate, was not to be seen.

On his fifth voyage, after having beaten off an attack at midnight by two Spanish armed boats under oars at the mouth of Campeachy harbour, Captain Little set sail, but shortly after was chased by the pirate Gibbs for a day and a night.

Our craft was dressed with all the canvas that could be set, and hauled up so that every sail would draw on the starboard tack. The pirate was no laggard. Hour after hour passed, and no perceptible difference was discovered in the sailing of the two vessels . . . At meridian it could not be ascertained that either vessel had the advantage in sailing; but the wind began to slacken its force, and as in a light breeze nothing that was ever built could probably sail faster than this beautiful craft, it became evident that she was stealing away from the pirate. Exasperated, no doubt, at the prospects of losing his prey, he opened a brisk cannonade upon us; but it was in vain, for every shot fell short of the schooner, and every discharge from his guns slackened his speed and gave us a corresponding advantage. At sunset we had gained about one mile . . .

Captain Little held the same course all night long, but when the breeze freshened at midnight, he was obliged to take in his studding sails.

At daylight, in the morning, the pirate was again a gunshot and a half, astern, under a cloud of canvas. Our studding sails were again set, but not without the expectation of losing the booms, sails, &c., as the wind blew strong, and our craft was bounding over the sea at the rate of twelve knots. It was a hard, although a most splendid chase, and I know not how it would have terminated, if we had not, at 10 o'clock, fallen in with the American man-of-war schooner *Shark*, which, when discovered by the pirate, caused him to take in sail, and haul upon a wind. The last we saw of him was in full flight from the man-of-war, although he appeared to outsail the *Shark* with ease.

The schooner was sold for a large sum in Havana and Captain Little returned by sea to Baltimore which he reached on 20 July 1826. In the *National Watercraft Collection*, Howard Chapelle writes that the fastest vessel in the American Navy at the end of the 1812-15 War and for some years afterwards was the brig *Spark*. Perhaps she was the vessel which succoured Captain Little and his crew. Could a lapse in memory be responsible for a misplaced letter, or were they really two different vessels? The exploits of George Little's schooner make fascinating reading and must have been repeated on many privateers that preyed on shipping across the entire North Atlantic.

This splendid stereo photograph was taken at Havana, Cuba, in 1860, and shows an unidentified schooner entering the harbour, with Morro Castle on the port bow. Whether or not she is of clipper-build cannot be determined but she looks like a survivor from the past. Worth noting is how the colour of both the main boom and the bowsprit changes from dark to white, once outside the hull. (Courtesy of the Peabody Museum of Salem)

JUST AS there were two classes of schooners in America in the eighteenth century –the larger sea-going variety with square canvas in addition to gaff sails and the smaller 'shallop-type' with only two gaff sails–so the same can be said for Great Britain. Examples of English shallops have already been given in Chapter 4 and now the larger ocean-going schooners can be examined.

One would like to think that the arrival of the Portuguese schooner *St Ann* caused a stir at Portsmouth in 1736, but it is impossible to tell as there is no evidence that her lines and sail plan were copied (see Chapter 3). The first schooner registered in the Royal Navy appears to have been the *Barbadoes* of 130 tons, which was built in Virginia and bought at Antigua in 1757. Then six Marblehead-built schooners were purchased in 1767-68 to protect the New England fisheries and two further schooners were actually ordered from yards in New York, namely the *Earl of Egmont* and *Sir Edward Hawke*.

The French lexicographer, Antoine Lescallier, stated in his *Vocabulaire des Termes de Marine* in 1777 that schooners were mostly used in England and America, and that the sails resembled the mainsail of a brigantine or cutter. He added that there were two or three jibs, a topsail on each mast, and a square sail to be set when running before the wind. Among the principal maritime writers, Falconer in England, Chapman in Sweden and Groenewegen in Holland, there was but a single engraving given by each of them of a schooner's sails, demonstrating that the rig was known but not used much. Most illustrations of the rig at that time allot a square

Wearing a British flag, this bluff-bodied schooner with a pink stern was etched by Pierre Ozanne c1770. The main topmast, the head of which appears unfinished, is fidded abaft the lower mast; she is shown drying her sails, and the bowsprit has been run in so that the gear beneath it is slack. (Private collection)

topsail on both fore and main masts, and also a topgallant if one is set. As in America, the gaffs had now increased in length to the proportions seen in the nineteenth century, and both bowsprits and jibbooms were often excessively long. A spritsail yard may have helped to stiffen these long spars stretching out beyond the stem head, but there must have been problems before the advent of the dolphin striker in the last quarter of the eighteenth century.

Illustrations of English-built schooners are rare before 1800 and Ozanne's engraving *c*1770 (page 34) shows what a cumbersome, roughly-built vessel with a pink stern could have looked like. Edward Gwyn made some drawings *c*1780 and one of these, entitled 'A Topsail Schooner', has square sails on each mast; the topsails are deeply roached and are sheeted to a spread yard set at some distance below the hounds; there is a spritsail from the bowsprit and three headsails. Daniel Brocklebank built his first schooner, the *Experiment*, in 1802 but twenty years were to elapse before his second one appeared. A cargo-carrying type may be seen in plans of one built for Port Jackson. This vessel is full-bodied with rounded bilges and not much deadrise; there are square topsails on each mast; the foresail has no boom, which was a common feature at that time. It should be noted that gaff or jib-headed topsails were not in common use before the end of the eighteenth century, although Thomas Luny sketched one in 1799 on a shallop , as may be seen in one of his sketch books at the National Maritime Museum.

Top right: The Alert, *seen here at Whitby, has the hull of a collier brig and with her round stern was probably a billy boy. Of 43 tons, she was built at Whitby in 1802. The topsail yard is hanging on its lifts from the lower mast cap, which was then a common practice on the north-east coast; the topgallant yard has been lowered below the cap so it could not have had a mast parral.* (Nautical Photo Agency)

Right: The venerable schooner Jane *was built at Pwllheli in 1827, and in 1879 measured 71.0ft x 17.3ft x 10.2ft and 94 tons. She had been lengthened in 1855 and again in 1869, and so had probably begun life as a sloop or galliot with only one mast. She had a round stern and is being steered with a tiller; a jib is set but is difficult to make out, owing to its light colour.* (Basil Lavis Collection)

In England, fast-sailing vessels were usually rigged as cutters with a broad beam, steep deadrise and fine lines, and some went up to 150 tons in size; sometimes the brig rig was given to a larger cutter hull-form. The schooner rig appears to have been applied to cargo-carrying craft where speed was unimportant, but where cheapness of outfit and small crews were desirable. The American version of a fast-sailing vessel was basically that of a longer and narrower hull-form to which a schooner rig was fitted with numerous square sails and many flying kites; by degrees the British came to adopt a modified type of schooner as an economical craft in peacetime, which was capable of performing many duties and was suitable for varying trades. Occasionally a cutter was cut in half, the bow and stern portions dragged apart, and a new centre section some 10ft to 15ft long was built in the gap. Presumably it was cheaper and quicker than building a new vessel.

To show the lack of interest in building schooners in the United Kingdom at the beginning of the nineteenth century, David Steel's folio of plans that accompanied his work, *Naval Architecture*, in the first edition of 1805 and two subsequent editions, does not include a single example of a British-built schooner, although there are three plans of American schooners. However, examples from shipyard records show

In Ilfracombe harbour are the smack Polly *(left) and the schooner* Charles Tucker. *The full-bodied schooner has a fairly flat bottom and only heels slightly as she takes the ground at low water. She was built at Swansea in 1839 by W Meager and measured 80.6ft x 20.4ft x 10.3ft and 160 tons net. Her last entry in* Lloyd's Register *was 1890 when she was owned in Penzance. She has a single topsail and topgallant clewed up on her tall foremast.* (Janette Rosing Photographic Archive)

that an interest in schooner-building had been awakened. At Lancaster in 1807, John Brockbank contracted to build a three-masted schooner with a length 'aloft' of 81ft 6in, extreme breadth of 21ft 0in and a tonnage of 153 tons at a cost of £10 10s per ton; unfortunately no spar dimensions are listed. Her builder described her as 'schooner'. This was the *Lancashire Witch* which was armed with four 9pdr and twelve 12pdr guns, and as Mr T Best was both master and owner she probably carried a Letter of Marque; in 1808 she voyaged to Barbados. *Lloyd's Register* gives her tonnage as 190. Another example of a schooner built about this time was the *Plough* of 86 tons, built by Alexander Hall in 1811 at a cost of £10 per ton. She had two masts, and spar dimensions are given in the firm's surviving records, with the exception of the mast spacings. A note reads: 'Fore boom and gaff to fit between masts'. There were square sails on both masts and the main yard was termed a 'crossjack yard'.

An important event occurred in 1830 with the publication of *A Treatise on Marine Architecture* written by Peter Hedderwick and published by himself in Edinburgh, consisting of a book of text and a portfolio of twenty-one plans of merchant vessels. For once, naval craft are excluded. Although only one vessel, the schooner *Charlotte*, is actually named in a description of the plates, several can be identified by studying the text. A unique feature of the plates is that there are actually three sail and rigging plans drawn, namely, a full-rigged ship of 500 tons, a topsail schooner and a

The Victoria *passing Elsinore, as painted by the Danish artist Jacob Petersen. She was built in Guernsey in 1837 and her lofty masts suggest a hull-form that was moderately full, and which needed a fair amount of canvas to propel it along. The original painting was made available to me for copying by J Attwood.*

*Lines plan and deck layout of
the* Glasgow, *redrawn and
reconstructed by the author
from Peter Hedderwick's*
Treatise on Marine
Architecture *(1830), plate
XVI. She was built at Leith in
1826. Reconstruction: deck
fittings in plan and elevation
from contemporary
illustrations.*

cutter. It seems highly probable that the topsail schooner was the *Glasgow* which
was designed by him and built at Leith in 1826 for trade between that port and
Hamburg. Her measurements were 72ft 0in (length for tonnage), 22ft 4in (breadth
for tonnage), 13ft 6in (depth of hold) and 155 tons. The lines plan has been redrawn
from Hedderwick's plate and the deck layout has been reconstructed, using the
spacing of the deck beams and contemporary illustrations. Like all his published
designs, the *Glasgow* was a deep, full-bodied craft with a full entrance and some
concavity in the run, and only slight deadrise with vertical sides. Hedderwick wrote
of her: 'She sails fast and carries a great cargo'.

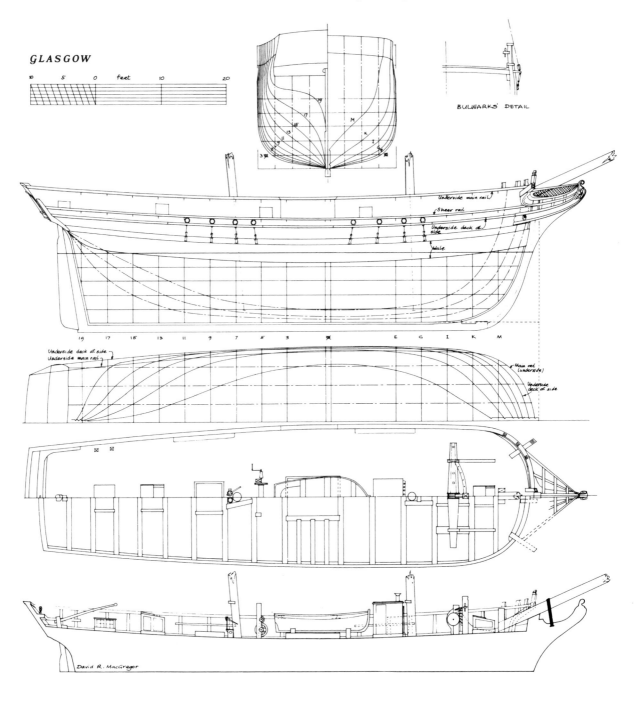

GLASGOW

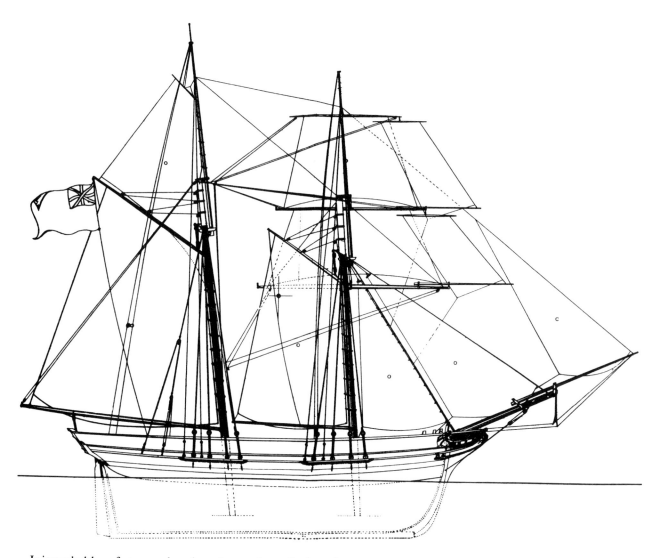

It is probably safe to say that there is no other sail plan of a merchant schooner in existence in Great Britain or America prior to this date which is so detailed, and for that reason it has not been redrawn but is reproduced as Hedderwick drew it. Other detailed plans, such as those drawn by myself, or by other persons in America, are reconstructions employing tables of spar dimensions and contemporary rules for rigging and sailmaking. An interesting point about the *Glasgow*'s sail plan is the method of rigging the topsail yard which here hoists on a parral on the topmast *below* the cap. The head of the lower mast has been specially lengthened for this reason and now measures 13ft above the cheeks while the comparable dimension of the mainmast is only 11ft. Normally, the head of each mast would be the same height. In this case, the topsail has considerably less hoist than the topgallant, and photographs show that when the latter needed to be furled, the yard was lowered close down on to the topsail and the crew could stand on the topsail yard footropes for their work. The advantages of this arrangement were that if the topmast had to be housed in a gale, the square topsail could still remain set, and as it did not have too much hoist, it did not have to be reefed. However, this form of rig was mostly

Sail plan of the Glasgow *reproduced from plate XXVI in Peter Hedderwick's* Treatise on Marine Architecture *(1830). See text for further comments.*

confined to ships of countries bordering either side of the North Sea and was most popular in the first half of the nineteenth century.

Other points about the *Glasgow*'s sail plan are that the ratlines are not drawn on the shrouds and that the latter set up on outside channels, whereas in many schooners the rigging set up on the main rail; the running backstay on the mainmast is prominent; the topping lift to the fore boom goes to the hounds of the mainmast, but is difficult to see as it almost coincides with one of the shrouds; the inclusion of studding sails on a schooner's sail plan is an interesting feature. A painting of the *Frankfort Packet* on page 54 depicts a very similar vessel to the *Glasgow*; in fact, she was built in 1818 and was owned by the same firm in Leith; perhaps she was even designed by Hedderwick himself. She has a royal set flying without any braces and has also hoisted up a square sail to her fore yard; the flying jib is set on a stay which the *Glasgow* does not have.

The design and construction of schooners must have been well-advanced by an illustration such as this one of the *Glasgow*, particularly as Hedderwick's book remained in use at many shipyards for the next thirty years.

Unidentified schooner with a sail plan similar to the Glasgow *except that there is a royal set here. The artist is unknown. This schooner is remarkably similar to the* Magnus Troil *of 124 tons which was built at Aberdeen in 1830; she was owned in Lerwick and her sail plan is reproduced on page 38 of the author's* Schooners in Four Centuries *(1982). (Courtesy of the Peabody Museum of Salem)*

Naval Schooners | 7

REFERENCE HAS already been made to schooners added to the Royal Navy either by capture or by purchase. Up to 1793, the captures were probably confined to American vessels, particularly privateers. During the Napoleonic Wars, American schooners continued to be captured, but now French schooners were also being taken and added to the Royal Navy as were a few from other European countries, but after 1815, captures were confined to a few slavers. Of purchased schooners prior to 1812, many were built to the order of the Admiralty in American shipyards. Plans drawn from some of the captured vessels inspired copies to be built, as already described in previous chapters. Up to the end of the Napoleonic Wars, the design and construction of schooners which were not influenced by American models is hard to trace, although it is fairly safe to say that any of cutter-build stem from a purely English development.

One such vessel is the *Helena*, date of launch unknown, but presumably built to obtain a Letter of Marque; she was bought by the Royal Navy early in 1778 and was captured by the French in September the same year; she was then re-captured in 1779 still bearing the name of *Helena*. She lasted in the Navy for nineteen years until she went missing in northern waters in 1798. Her lines were taken off in 1778 and the official dimensions, which vary slightly with those on the take-off, were 76ft 1.5in length on deck, 26ft 9in extreme breadth, 10ft 8in depth of hold and 214 $^{84}\!/_{94}$ tons or 220 tons. She had a crew of seventy to eighty men and was armed with fourteen 6pdr guns. Her plan shows her to have great rise of floor with the maxi-

Sail plan of HMS Helena *entirely reconstructed by the author from spar dimensions listed on an Admiralty draught in the National Maritime Museum, London. Not given in this list of spars: head yard to square foresail, lengths of doublings of each mast and of jibboom.*

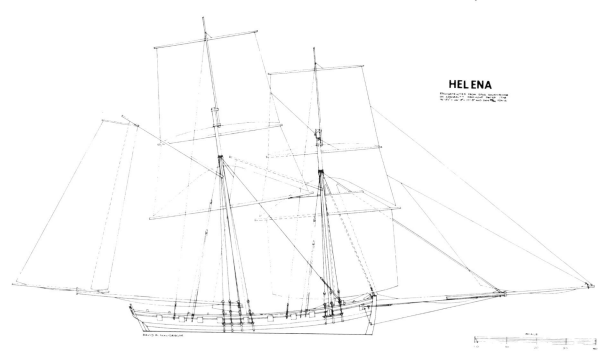

HELENA

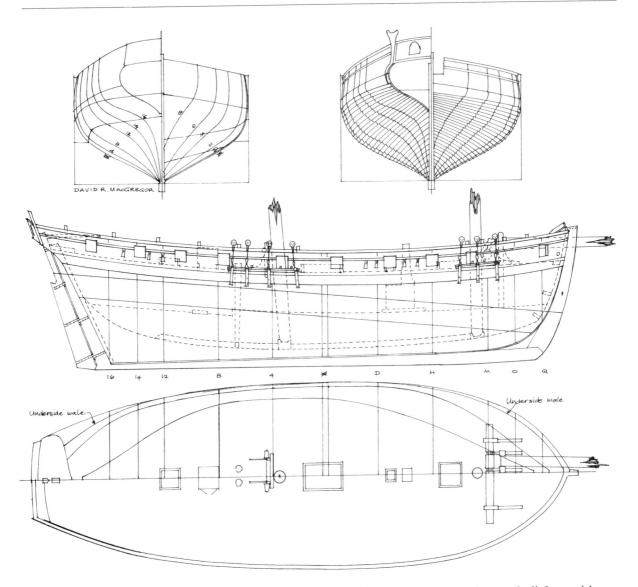

DAVID R. MACGREGOR

Underside wale

Underside wale

Lines, deck layout and planking of HMS *Helena redrawn by the author from an Admiralty draught at the National Maritime Museum, London. Built 1778. Reconstruction: deck plan combined here from a separate draught.*

mum beam above the load line which is the conventional cutter hull-form with convex waterlines and drag aft. She drew 13ft 9in aft and 7ft 0in forward. In spite of her broad hull with a ratio of only three beams to length, she has a narrow stern with a square tuck. From the bow and stern end elevations, it will be noticed that she had clinker planking up to the wales and then was carvel-planked above, which is a style of construction to be found on several one- and two-masted craft acquired by the Navy at about this time. The deck layout has been reconstructed from another plan and the longitudinal section has the galley range and funnel drawn. She was fitted with a windlass which was normal for merchant vessels but in the Navy was only found in smaller craft.

The list of spar dimensions appeared on her draught in 1778 and so were presumably those she had when purchased. Three yards are listed for each mast— spread yard, topsail yard and topgallant yard; however, no topmast is listed, only a 'topgallant mast', which is a practice often to be found in spar dimensions of cutters at this date. The reconstruction of the sail plan from this list of spars has proved a problem, with so few examples of English schooners to consult, and after trying various arrangements, the most logical solution was to fit a cutter's rig on each mast. Accordingly, the rig of the cutter HMS *Fly* (below) has been used to work out the sail plan: the topsail yards have been crossed on the head of the lower masts; the foot of each topsail is deeply roached and the spread yard is a long way below the hounds; the topgallant masts, which have been fidded on the fore side of the lower masts, are used to set a sail of square proportions with a big hoist; the head of the square foresail is laced to a yard and hoisted up close to the foot of the topsail. The resulting plan inevitably bears a close affinity to the schooner drawn by Edward Gwyn *c*1780. On *Helena*, the stem head is drawn with holes bored through to take the fantail end of a stay, and so the fore stay is set up here. I have drawn two headsails from stays taken to the hounds and the flying jib stay goes to the head of the topgallant mast. The lengths of the spars are prodigious, with a main boom 54ft 5in long, a ringtail boom of 33ft 9in, a bowsprit of 56ft 5in and a jibboom of 50ft. No doubt there would have been studdingsails on the foremast and presumably the full suit of sails would only have been set in very light breezes, although the great breadth of beam would have provided some stability.

After 1815, there were no American schooners to capture and add to the Royal Navy, and the Admiralty was obliged to order some and purchase others. They were employed in the Coastguard and Revenue service, for surveying and as mail packets. Sir Robert Seppings designed the three-masted packet schooner *Seagull* which was built in 1829 with dimensions given on the plan of 95ft 0in length on deck, 26ft

Below: Sail plan of HMS Fly *reconstructed by the author from spar dimensions listed on an Admiralty draught in the National Maritime Museum, Greenwich. This cutter was bought into the Royal Navy in 1763; measurements given on draught were 51ft 6in (overall) x 20ft 10½in (extreme) x 8ft 1¼in and 78 tons.*

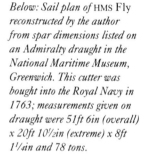

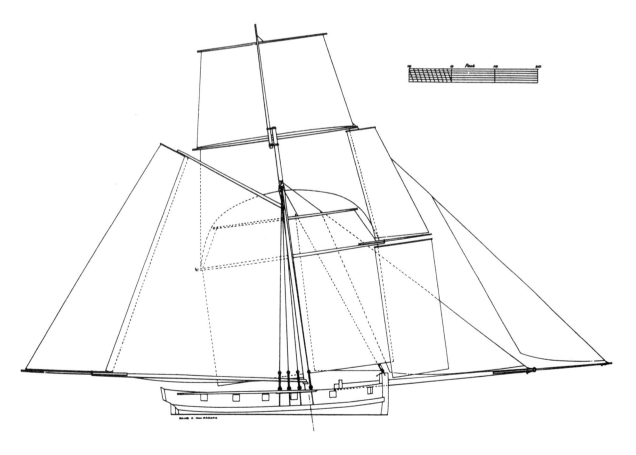

This painting by Thomas Buttersworth (1768-1842) entitled 'Shipping in the Tagus' has, in the foreground, a heavily-rigged schooner-brigantine with a three-piece foremast on which there are four yards, but also a large gaff sail. This illustrates the amount of canvas that could be set, and includes studding sails, ringtail and two main topmast staysails. (Courtesy of the Parker Gallery)

3in extreme breadth, 11ft 2in depth of hold and 279 tons. In drawing out the lines plan opposite, I have simplified it somewhat by reducing the number of stations and omitting the chain plates and deadeyes. Her hull-form is really a lengthened version of a cutter's hull with hollow garboards, steep deadrise, slack bilges, maximum beam above the load line, convex waterlines and some hollow in the run. The lofty sail plan is reminiscent of the American three-masted schooner *Revenge*, taken into the Royal Navy in 1806 as the *Flying Fish*, in which the fore and main lower masts are very long, making the gaff sails tall and narrow, with square topsails above them on diminutive topmasts.

Amongst the Admiralty Collection of draughts at the National Maritime Museum, there is a very detailed sail and rigging plan of HMS *Hornet*, dated 1828, which combines a longitudinal section and elevations of the deck fittings with the external profile superimposed; all the standing rigging is carefully drawn with the exception of the ratlines; but the running rigging is incomplete, because although the gaff and throat halliards are drawn, and also the sheets of the square fore topsail,

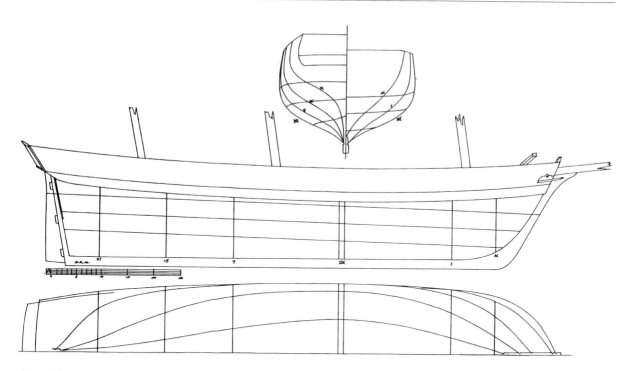

Above: Lines plan of HMS Seagull *(built 1831) redrawn by the author from Admiralty draught in the National Maritime Museum, London. Some of the stations have been omitted to simplify the plan.*

Below: Outline sail plan of HMS Seagull *redrawn by Janette Rosing from an Admiralty draught in the National Maritime Museum, London, which had this sail plan and that of a brig combined on one sheet.*

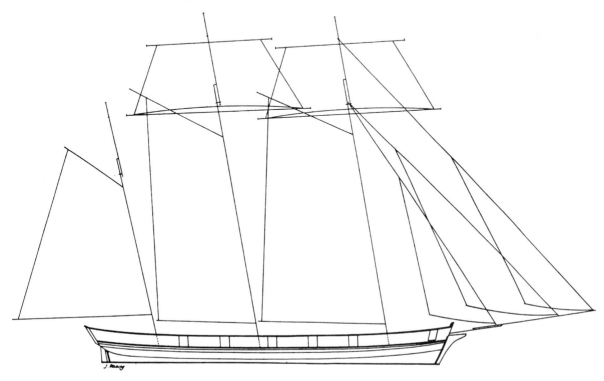

A model made by Mr F Hinchliffe of HMS *Hornet, built in 1831 at Chatham. Of 181 tons builder's measurement, she measured 81ft length and 23.5ft breadth and mounted six guns. She was broken up in 1845. (Edward Bowness)*

no other sheets are drawn nor are there any braces to the three yards on the foremast. Nevertheless, it is a welcome sight to find such a carefully-drawn plan in existence. There are a number of other Admiralty plans of schooners in the collection at the National Maritime Museum, covering the first half of the nineteenth century, and the amount of detail drawn on the deck plans is more carefully detailed than previously.

Correspondence in *The Mariner's Mirror* (Vol II, 1912) provides names of some of the last schooners in the Royal Navy which were said to be the *Alacrity, Beagle, Conflict, Renard* and *Sandfly* on the Australian station, and all of 120 tons old measurement. Thomas de Hoghton wrote that he had commanded the *Beagle* from 1877 to 1881 and found her a good sea boat 'but not good for sailing' and very uncertain when going about. Sweeps were carried and often used when negotiating narrow passages between coral reefs, boarding nettings were carried as a defence against pirates and there were frequent landings to replenish the water and gather wood for fires, as only 1 ton of coal was carried.

On the Jamaica station there was a schooner engaged in surveying. She had been purchased in the West Indies by the Admiralty in September 1877 under the name of *Lark*, ex-*Falcon*; she was renamed *Sparrowhawk* three months after she was bought. She survived until 1889 when she was sold in Bermuda. Three other schooners were on the Australian station from 1885-88, ostensibly for suppression of the slave trade; two of them were the *Harrier* and *Undine*, ex-*Morna* which were both purchased by the Admiralty in March 1881 and sold in Sydney in April 1888, and were rumoured to have been yachts. A third was the *Lark*, built by Westacott at Barnstaple in 1880, presumably to Admiralty order; she was sold at Sydney in 1887. In future it was the screw gunboat, albeit with the rig of a three-masted schooner, that was assigned to the work formerly carried out by the sailing schooners.

Pencil drawing entitled: 'J.C. 1820. HM Schooner Augusta. *Tender to* HMS Amphion *off Bus. Ay.'. Presumably off Buenos Ayres. The leech of the foresail is visible because the mainsail tack has been hauled up; there is a topmast studding sail set abaft the fore topsail; only two shrouds on the foremast and but one on the main suggest a small craft.* (MacGregor Collection)

8 | *Schooner-Brigantines*

IF A two-masted sailing vessel with conventional gaff sails on each mast and the usual number of headsails set on a bowsprit carries lower, topsail, topgallant and royal yards on the foremast and if the mast is in two pieces with a lower mast and fidded topmast, then it is fully acceptable to class her as a 'schooner'. But if that part of the foremast on which the topgallant and royal yards are crossed be a separately fidded mast—in fact, a topgallant mast—and if all the gaff sails remain as before, is she then still a schooner?

This three-piece mast is what the purists call a 'square-rigged' mast. But if the fore and main lower masts are of approximately equal height and no fore course is bent on the fore yard, is the three-piece foremast really a properly square-rigged mast? Should the vessel then be called a brigantine or a schooner?

It is this very rig variation which is used by Arthur Young to illustrate his definition of the word 'Schooner' in his *Nautical Dictionary*, first published at Dundee in 1846, as illustrated opposite.

Returning to the case of the vessel with the three-piece foremast, northern Europeans had a useful name for this sort of rig which they called *schunerbrigg* or 'schoonerbrig'. They also embraced under this category what we in Britain would call a 'brigantine'. Perhaps our terminology should be 'schooner-brigantine' but whatever the name it makes an attractive and very effectual rig. There is a good balance between square and fore-and-aft canvas: the vessel could point up into the wind as well as a schooner, but with a fair wind on the quarter or from astern she had a complete mast of square canvas which was augmented with studdingsails on each side. In his *Treatise on Masting Ships* (2nd edition 1843), John Fincham has a table for two-masted vessels termed 'brig forward and schooner aft' which produces a rig

A painting signed by Honoré Pellegrin of Marseilles which depicts the Scotia *entering the harbour there in 1845, two years after she was built. The foremast is clearly a three-piece mast with four yards, the fore square sail being sheeted to a bentinck boom. She was a broad deep vessel with dimensions of 69.4ft x 18.6ft x11.1ft and 135 tons.* (Courtesy of the Parker Gallery)

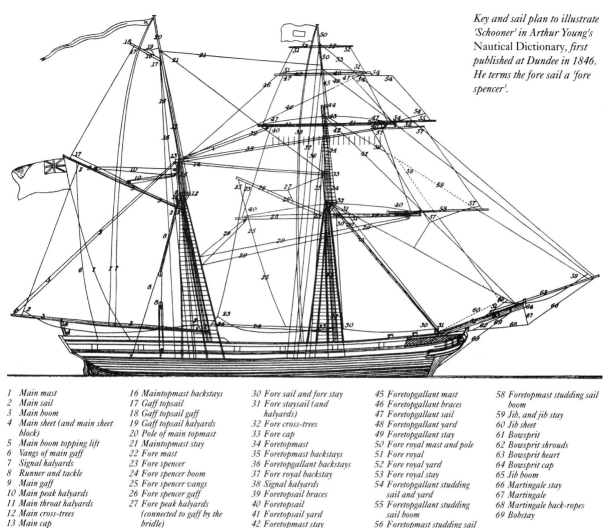

Key and sail plan to illustrate 'Schooner' in Arthur Young's Nautical Dictionary, *first published at Dundee in 1846. He terms the fore sail a 'fore spencer'.*

1 Main mast
2 Main sail
3 Main boom
4 Main sheet (and main sheet block)
5 Main boom topping lift
6 Vangs of main gaff
7 Signal halyards
8 Runner and tackle
9 Main gaff
10 Main peak halyards
11 Main throat halyards
12 Main cross-trees
13 Main cap
14 Main stay
15 Main topmast

16 Maintopmast backstays
17 Gaff topsail
18 Gaff topsail gaff
19 Gaff topsail halyards
20 Pole of main topmast
21 Maintopmast stay
22 Fore mast
23 Fore spencer
24 Fore spencer boom
25 Fore spencer vangs
26 Fore spencer gaff
27 Fore peak halyards (connected to gaff by the bridle)
28 Fore yard
29 Fore braces

30 Fore sail and fore stay
31 Fore staysail (and halyards)
32 Fore cross-trees
33 Fore cap
34 Foretopmast
35 Foretopmast backstays
36 Foretopgallant backstays
37 Fore royal backstay
38 Signal halyards
39 Foretopsail braces
40 Foretopsail
41 Foretopsail yard
42 Foretopmast stay
43 Foretopmast cross-trees
44 Foretopmast cap

45 Foretopgallant mast
46 Foretopgallant braces
47 Foretopgallant sail
48 Foretopgallant yard
49 Foretopgallant stay
50 Fore royal mast and pole
51 Fore royal
52 Fore royal yard
53 Fore royal stay
54 Foretopgallant studding sail and yard
55 Foretopgallant studding sail boom
56 Foretopmast studding sail yard
57 Foretopmast studding sail

58 Foretopmast studding sail boom
59 Jib, and jib stay
60 Jib sheet
61 Bowsprit
62 Bowsprit shrouds
63 Bowsprit heart
64 Bowsprit cap
65 Jib boom
66 Martingale stay
67 Martingale
68 Martingale back-ropes
69 Bobstay

that is roughly equivalent to the European term. Nautical terminology was not then so strict which was probably just as well, considering the many rig variations, and ships were not assigned to the rigid categories that became the case in the twentieth century.

The schooner-brigantine was popular from the 1820s for about sixty years or so, but especially in the first half of the nineteenth century. In the United Kingdom and northern Europe, hulls were still heavy and somewhat cumbersome without much deadrise, and cargo-carrying was all-important. For voyages to collect fresh fruit from the Azores or dried fruit from the Mediterranean, a faster form of craft was needed to prevent deterioration of the cargo, and also to avoid seizure by pirates. A long 9pdr gun on a pivot was a regular armament, as well as muskets and pikes for the crew. The large sail area was effectual in making fast passages and consequently the rig was also popular amongst opium clippers.

The 'schooner packet' *St Helena*, built in 1814 at the Blackwall Yard on the Thames for the Honourable East India Company, was an early example of a schooner-brigantine. She was employed to take supplies to the island in the South Atlantic after which she was named, and the lines plan below exhibits a short deep hull with a convex entrance and a run with some hollow in the lower body, some rise of floor with rounded bilges and fairly vertical sides without much tumblehome, a square stern and a plain bow with a gammon knee. Dimensions on the plan at the National Maritime Museum give 75ft 0in length on deck, 20ft 7in beam, 13ft 0in depth in hold and 135 20/94 tons. The length on deck actually scales 81ft 3in, which is what is drawn here. Her cost was £21 per ton and her duties were to attend East Indiamen visiting the island. The deck layout is partly on the lines plan and the elevations are on the sail plan. Abaft the foremast, there was a launch standing on chocks on the deck with the boat lying inside it, and a gig was slung from stern davits.

There had to be some reconstruction on the sail plan as the length of the fore topgallant mast was not listed, nor was the head of the fore lower mast, the royal yard, the spritsail yard and the flying jibboom. The spar dimensions given on the original plan suggest that she was designed to be a topgallant yard schooner, but that later she was fitted with a separately fidded topgallant mast. The spars and sails drawn here are all referred to in the log-book for the period 1819-22. As the ex-American privateer HMS *Sea Lark* has virtually the same length on deck as the

Lines and deck layout of the St Helena *redrawn by the author from plans at the National Maritime Museum, London. Built at Blackwall Yard, London, in 1814. Reconstruction: plan view of deck fittings, including windlass, channels, stern davits and studding sail boom. Elevation of deck fittings are on longitudinal section.*

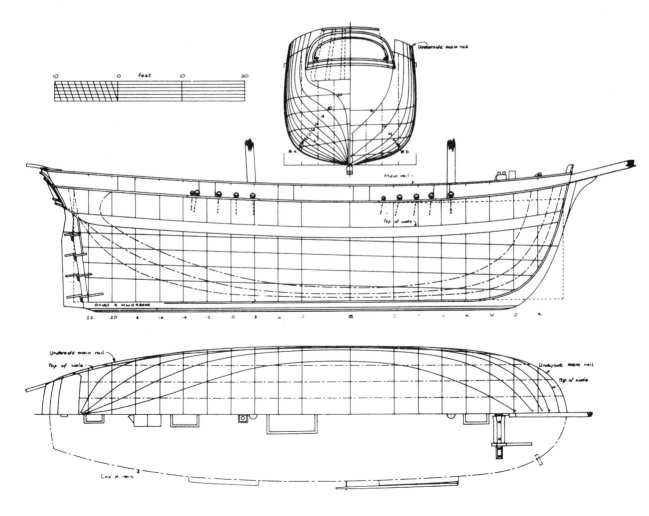

St Helena, it is worthwhile comparing the sail plans of the two vessels, to observe how the two builders coped with the differing requirements of each vessel.

Between 1814 and 1819, under the command of John Augustus Atkinson, the *St Helena* made eight round-trips between Cape Town and St Helena, carrying sheep, bullocks and various supplies such as wine and grain to the Island, and returning back empty; once she sailed to Benguela and loaded bullocks there.

One of the log-books opens with her refitting at St Helena in June 1819 and discharging bags of grain; the rigging to the lower masts was sent ashore to refit on 21 June but was re-fitted on 1 July. After the topmasts to each mast were fidded again, the *St Helena* was 'careened' for the carpenter to repair the copper sheathing on the starboard side, but it does not state how far she was hove down or how it was done. Meanwhile, other work went on aboard and after five days, the log-book reads, 'Righted the schooner'. (This entry contains the name of the rig.) The topsail yard was crossed, the rigging was rattled down and the log records on 7 July that the crew 'fidded the fore-top-g-mast and got the flying jib boom out'. It seems unlikely that she was intended to be given a fidded fore topgallant mast at the time the list of spars was tabulated on the draught, else the wording would have been different. Nevertheless, the log-book has frequent references to new spars being made, such as: 'received a spare jib boom for a new main boom', 'carpenter making a new main

Sail plan and longitudinal section of the St Helena *showing the two lower masts of equal height and a fidded fore topgallant mast. This plan was reconstructed by the author from spar dimensions listed on the lines plan, although the lengths of topgallant mast, royal yard, spritsail yard and flying jibboom were omitted. Sails and rigging based on vessel's log-books and contemporary books on rigging and sailmaking.*

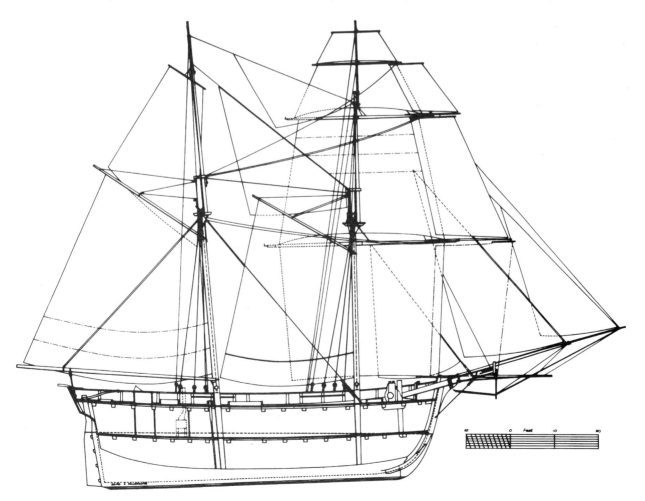

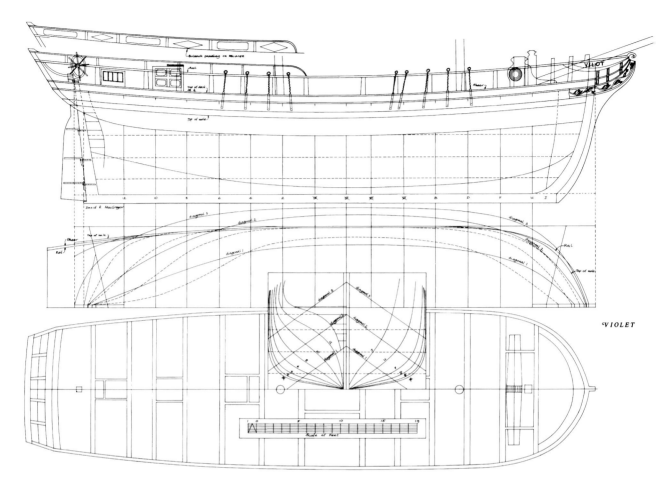

VIOLET

Lines and deck beams plan of
Violet *redrawn by the author*
from tracing he made of
builder's plan in the Science
Museum, London. Built at
Garmouth in 1839.

boom', 'carpenter making a sprit sail yard out of old main boom', so that it is entirely possible that the rig was changed from time to time after the schooner took up
her station in the South Atlantic.

The log-book only once mentions a royal yard with the words, 'Bent flying jib
and royal', suggesting it was a light-weather sail, and was possibly fitted without
braces which was the practice in many small vessels. There are frequent references
to setting and taking off the bonnet from the foresail.

On 2 August 1819 in a hard squall when bound to Cape Town on her ninth
trip, the *St Helena* 'carried away fore and main topmasts, flying jibboom and fore
top-g-mast, split the gaff foresail, main topmast staysail and top-g-sail'. After
clearing away the wreck, the following day they 'carried away the main sheet boom
and outer guy, repaired them and set the whole mainsail'. Two days after losing her
topmasts, new ones were fidded and the topsail and [fore] 'square sail' were set.

While beating into her anchorage at Cape Town on 11 August, she grounded in
the Bay on a hard, sandy bottom but got off by throwing all sails aback and drifted
off amongst the shipping. She immediately dropped her best bower anchor, but the
cable parted. Then she let go her small bower anchor and brought up against the
schooner *Uitenhague*, losing her starboard stern davit and lower studding sail boom,
but quickly bending her best bower cable to the spare anchor she wore round and
brought up in 2.5 fathoms. The harbour master's launch managed to pick up the

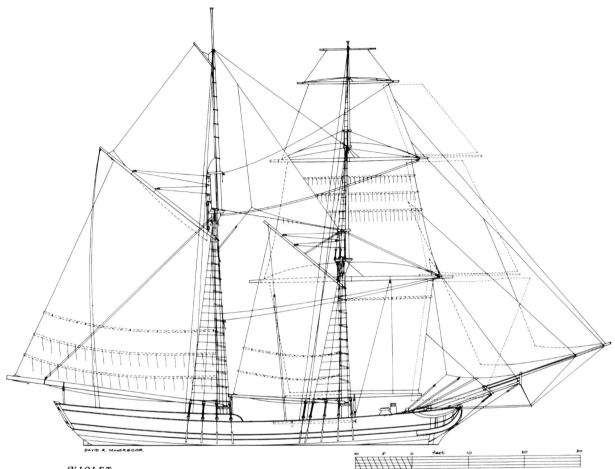

VIOLET

best bower anchor on the following day. On this passage from St Helena in 1819, she took twenty-four days to reach Cape Town and her best day's run was 183 miles, during which the highest speed was 8 knots. With a load line length of 77ft, a speed of 8 knots results in a speed-length ratio of 0.91.

Early the following month, partitions were erected in the 'tween decks in order to carry sheep to St Helena, and 134 were loaded together with 4 horses. She sailed a day later on 8 September, and reached the Island in twelve days, making four consecutive runs of 158, 172, 180 and 139 miles. On a later voyage, after levelling the hold with sand, she loaded 128 sheep and 17 bullocks. The carpenter shaped new spars and fished sprung ones though he was 'sick from frequent intoxication'. The method used to destroy rats on board was to light four charcoal fires in the hold, batten down the hatches and wait for a day, after which the hatches could be opened and the bodies be removed.

The schooner left St Helena for London on 22 September 1821 and in addition to her crew there were twenty-three soldiers, eight women and nineteen children, as well as a woman passenger and her child. The Lizard Light was seen thirty-eight days later and Dungeness was passed on 5 November, after a passage of forty-four days.

A new master was appointed in 1822 to succeed Atkinson. He was James Faifax, and his crew and their wages for a new commission were as follows:

Sail plan of the Violet *reconstructed by the author from spar dimensions listed on the lines plan. Sails and rigging based on contemporary books on sailmaking and rigging, and on ship portraits. Lengths of doublings and yard arms not listed on plan.*

The Frankfort Packet *of 127
tons carried four yards on her
foremast, but as the parral of
the topsail yard slid on the
doubling, the sail was not as
deep as the topgallant. She was
built at Leith in 1818, and this
portrait of her was painted by
F Albinus of Hamburg.*
(Courtesy of the Parker
Gallery)

Master	£30 per month
Chief mate	£15 per month
Second mate	£10 per month
Boatswain	£5 per month
Carpenter	£5 per month
Eight seamen	£2.10s per month
Landsman	£2 per month

Unfortunately, no contemporary illustration has been found of the *St Helena*,
although several views of the island have been examined in case she had been
included amongst the shipping pictured there.

Ideally, the schooner-brigantine should have both lower masts of equal height,
like the *St Helena*, but there were innumerable cases in which the fore lower mast
was shorter than that on the main, as in the case of the *Violet* whose plans are given
here. They were traced from a builder's plan in the Science Museum, London.
This rig is more of a brigantine than a schooner but it is worth while having an
example to compare both versions. The *Violet* was a small and broad vessel, built in
1839 at Garmouth by James Geddie of 74 tons old measurement and dimensions of
62ft 0in length, 18ft 9in beam (moulded) and 9ft 0in depth (approx). She had a full

hull-form with not much deadrise; the deck fittings have been reconstructed from the deck beams plan, and the sail plan has been reconstructed from a list of spar dimensions on the builder's lines plan. This was a very common form of rig in the first half of the nineteenth century, although the fitting of a bentinck boom was less common.

A few schooners were built in the nineteenth century with four yards on each mast, one of which was the *Amy Stockdale*. A print, published in 1839, depicts her under sail off Dover setting a large gaff sail and a square topsail on each mast; the topgallants on each mast were clewed up and no royal yards were crossed. Although no square sail was bent on the fore yard, one was undoubtedly available in fair winds. Another of this type was the *Dorothea* of 182 tons, built at Nordby, Denmark, 1869-70. According to a photograph in *Fanø-Sejlskibe* by Frode Holm-Petersen, she resembled the *Amy Stockdale* except that staysails from the mainmast replaced the fore gaff sail. In 1829, Alexander Hall at Aberdeen contracted to build the *Matilda* with the rig of 'schooner or hermaphrodite'.

Other examples from southwest England and elsewhere show that the sort of rig described in this chapter was sometimes carried on a three-piece and sometimes on a two-piece mast, and that the permutations were too great to be covered by a hard-and-fast definition.

Some vessels like the Lizzie Garrow *did not have a fidded topgallant mast, and in order to stiffen the long topmast, crosstrees were fitted with appropriate rigging as illustrated here. She was built by Date at Kingsbridge in 1854 with a length of 92.6ft and was of 218 tons o.m. and 174 tons n.m. She traded to the West Indies and Mediterranean.* (Fairweather Collection by courtesy of Malcolm Darch)

9 | *Clipper Schooners*

Lines and sail plan of the Swedish schooner Zaritza, drawn and reconstructed by Ralph Bird from an old plan once owned by Percy Dalton. Built at Bergen in 1857; length of waterline 97ft 9in, breadth 24ft 9in, 270 tons o.m. She was a comparatively shallow draught vessel, but her large beam made her stiff enough to carry this large sail area. When the ice melted in the Baltic, she used to race fresh fruit back to Sweden.

THE EVOLUTION and development of the fine-lined, fast-sailing British cutter as a precursor of the clipper in the United Kingdom is now well-established; and even when the cutter's rig of an enormous gaff sail, numerous headsails, additional square canvas and an assortment of flying kites – all supported on a single mast – was replaced by the two masts of schooner or brig, nothing much more was often achieved than a rig variation on an immense cutter's hull. Yet a change was gradually appearing.

The broad, short proportions of the cutter were influenced by an Act of Parliament in 1784 which specified a maximum beams-to-length ratio of 3.5:1 for cutters, luggers, shallops and other such craft and which was still law in 1833. Its intention was to curb the smuggling habit, although square-rigged vessels or sloops with standing bowsprits were excused. Licences were obtainable for legitimate trade to avoid seizure by the Customs or Revenue Service.

British schooners were thus greatly influenced by the cutter's hull-form which was basically lengthened without increasing the breadth. The Bristol yard of J M

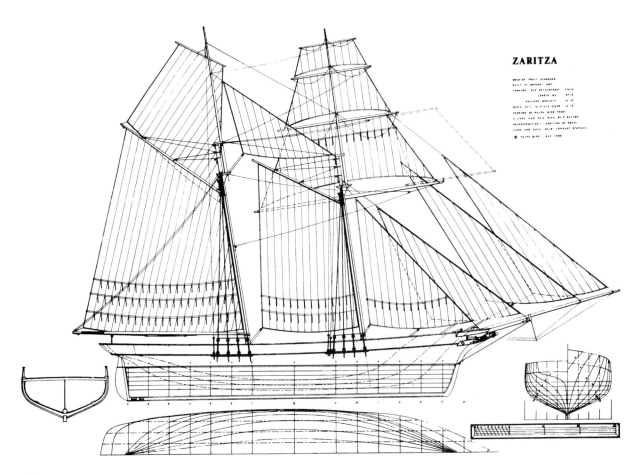

ZARITZA

Hilhouse built or designed six schooners in the ten years after 1815, of which the *Sappho* is easiest to study as her plan is identifiable. Length scaled off the plan, foreside of stem to afterside of sternpost along the rabbet, is 83ft 6in, which is apparently 5ft longer than when the vessel was built, due to alteration in 1824. Breadth was 20ft 4in and depth of hold 11ft 4in, resulting in 145 tons. There are no spar dimensions. She was advertised in 1822 as having made one voyage to Smyrna and was a 'new and very fast sailing schooner'. Her lines plan, reproduced as figure 60 in the author's *Fast Sailing Ships* (1st ed. 1973), shows a vessel with very steep deadrise, and having an easy convex entrance and a fine hollow run. The midship section is placed well forward, and the dotted line around the hull indicates how the stem, keel, sternpost and sheer have been reconstructed. She is probably the earliest British fruit schooner for which plans have been discovered. Her ratio of four beams to length, together with a depth of hold that is only slightly more than half the breadth, resulted in a hull of long and shallow proportions which was infrequently seen in England at this date. No doubt her schooner rig included three or four yards for square sails on the foremast. She survived until 1827.

American clipper schooners would have been seen and studied by English shipbuilders, but what they thought of them is now unknown. Suffice it is to say that the cutter hull-form remained as a dominant influence for another two decades. A

A watercolour of an unknown schooner which was captured off Havana, Cuba, on 26 July 1858 by HMS Lapwing *with 500 slaves aboard. The artist was Captain Montague Reilly RN who wrote the above details on the painting, adding that the schooner was built of mahogany. Each mast was a pole without a doubling. (MacGregor Collection)*

shipbuilder usually believed that he could excel by his design the hull of the vessel he was observing, even though he might enter notes about her in his private journal. The hull-form of the clipper brig *Anonyma* exhibited some cutter influence when built in 1839.

Another type of schooner was developed from the brig by merely altering the rig whereby gaff sails were substituted for the square courses and the lower masts were increased in length. The schooner-brigantine *St Helena*, described in Chapter 8, is an example of this, and a schooner rig on the hull of a fine-lined brig is not illogical. Indeed, the increasing number of schooners must have had such hull-forms, rather than having a specially-designed hull. By the 1830s, the expansion of the opium trade between India and China, the growing enthusiasm for yachting, the increasing fondness for fresh oranges, lemons and other fruit, and the desire for faster conveyance in the coastal packets for passengers and mail, all encouraged the designing and building of fast-sailing vessels for which the schooner rig was eminently suitable.

By 1835, Great Britain had treaties with Portugal, Spain, Brazil and France which

A watercolour signed 'Thomas G. Dutton' and painted in 1847 depicting two opium clippers near the Chusan Archipelago off the China coast in 1841. On the left is the brig Ann, *which was an ex-slaver of 252 tons captured in 1834 with a length of 101ft and a beam of 24ft. The other is the schooner* Lyra *of 165 tons which entered the trade in 1841. She is shown with a large area of canvas set but her straight stem is unusual.*
(Courtesy of James Dickie)

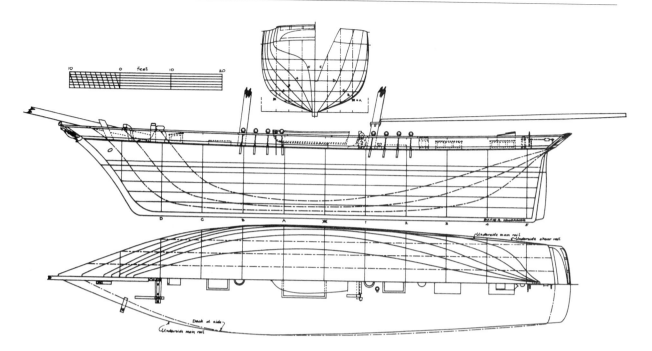

Lines and deck layout of the Scottish Maid *of 142 tons n.m. drawn and reconstructed by the author from the builder's half-model which at one time was in possession of the Glasgow Museum and Art Gallery. Built at Aberdeen in 1839. The figurehead, mast positions and all the deck fittings were reconstructed.*

Sail and rigging plan of the Scottish Maid *drawn and reconstructed by the author with the assistance of James Henderson. Sources: spar dimensions listed in builder's cost account book, contemporary books on sailmaking and rigging, paintings of other Aberdeen schooners.*

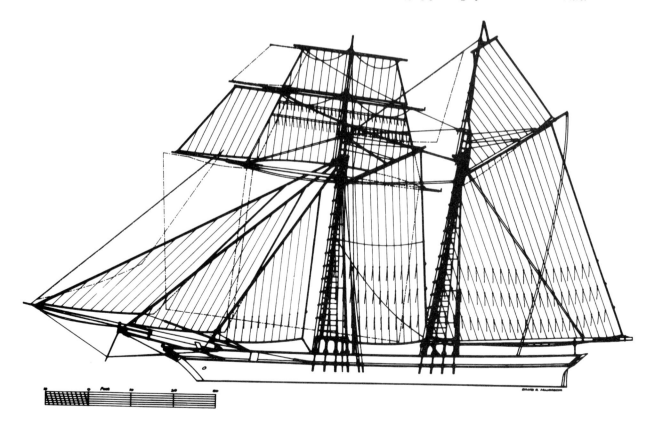

The three-masted schooner
Huntress *of 175 tons, here
pictured entering Malta
harbour, was built at Salcombe
in 1862 by Vivian. She had a
length of 109ft, and was a lofty
vessel with a royal on the
foremast.* (Fairweather
Collection by courtesy of
Malcolm Darch)

enabled the Royal Navy to stop, search and even seize any of their vessels which
were carrying slaves or were suspected of carrying them, but it had been impossible
to negotiate anything with the United States. Accordingly, the American flag provided a sort of safe conduct to vessels engaged in this trade as far as Havana or
Brazil, but for the run to the African coast and when slaves were on board, they flew
their true national colours. Many schooners and brigs were built in and around
Baltimore for this trade in the years 1830-60.

Some fine-lined slavers were captured by the Royal Navy during this period and
one, the *Theresa Secunda*, which was built at Philadelphia in 1831, had 460 slaves on
board when taken in 1832 by the brig HMS *Pelorus*, when under the Spanish flag.
She was sold to become a yacht under the ownership of the Hon R F Greville with
the name of *Xarifa*. Howard Chapelle used a plan of her in *The Search for Speed under
Sail* which showed that she had a long shallow hull, with large deadrise and sharp
convex waterlines with dimensions of 90ft 8in length, 21ft 11in breadth, 9ft 6in
depth and 177 tons. Her listed spar dimensions indicate that the foremast was only
2ft shorter than the mainmast, and that she crossed three yards on the foremast,
making her a topsail schooner.

Fine-lined schooners were wanted in the opium trade and many were rigged as
schooner-brigantines. The need to beat up the China Sea against the northeast
monsoon was paramount in their design, but powerful vessels were required to
withstand gales and typhoons, and they had to be well-armed to protect themselves
against pirates. Some were especially built for the trade, but former yachts, fruiters

and ex-naval craft were all to be found on the China coast. Masters of the opium clippers were highly paid. When Alick J Ryrie was in temporary command of Jardine Matheson's 175-ton schooner *Mazeppa* in 1852, he was getting £50 per month. A year later, when he obtained command of the brig *Audax*, his brother Phineas wrote home to their sister in Liverpool: 'As captain of a clipper he is a big swell, quite a Prince compared with the skipper of one of the ordinary description of merchant vessels'.

A lively account of the opium clipper *Eamont* was written by Lindsay Anderson, her third officer, and published under the title of *A Cruise in an Opium Clipper*. She was built at Cowes by White in 1852 and was of 120 tons with a length of 87ft and a beam of 20ft. She was armed with four 18pdrs and two pivot guns, and had a crew of about forty. Needless to say, the size of everything had increased somewhat in Anderson's memory, so that he allots a length to the main boom which is 23ft longer than the schooner herself. But it was obviously a long spar and undoubtedly 'a swinger and needed some handling'. The sail set from the fore yard is termed a 'balloon-squaresail' and the gaff foresail is a 'fore trysail'. There is a good story of sailing through the surf into the harbour of Taku in Formosa and bumping across the reef in the process, and also of attacks by war junks.

The firm of J & R White were notable shipbuilders of clipper ships, steamers and also of smaller craft, including cutters and schooners. Some idea of the continued

The Dartmouth-built schooner King of Tyre, depicted in 1837 whilst passing Gibraltar when bound from Messina to London, had been built the previous year of 82 tons to class 12 A1. With four square sails on the foremast, two studding sails set and the clew of the square sail hauled out by a passaree boom, she sets as much square canvas as a brigantine. (Fairweather Collection by courtesy of Malcolm Darch)

The significance of two vessels together in a painting usually indicates some common ground, and the reason in this case is because both the vessels were owned in Limerick. The brig lowering her skysails is the Minstrel Boy of 244 tons which Balley of Shoreham built in 1839; the schooner is the Harriet of 186 tons, which is assumed to be the one built at Southampton in 1834. The Rock of Gibraltar is on the right and the artist is W J Huggins. A sailor on the Harriet, by the fore rigging, is in the act of hauling up her signal flags. (Courtesy of the Parker Gallery)

influence of the cutter hull-form on design principles can be judged by an extract from *Theory and Practice of Shipbuilding* (2nd ed. 1851) by Thomas White Jnr:

We find that the exact midship section of the *Harriet* cutter yacht, built some twenty years since for the Marquis Donegal, then Lord Belfast, was extended and adopted in the *Waterwitch* brig, of 330 tons; and the same has been carried out in the *Daring*, of 450 tons, or sufficiently so for the illustration of this point.

The *Harriet*, a 96-ton cutter, was owned by Lord Belfast as a member of the Royal Yacht Squadron from 1825 to 1828.

So far, examples of schooners built in the United Kingdom have come from the south or southwest of the country, but in Scotland there was to be a reappraisal of schooner design, beginning in 1839 with the launch from Alexander Hall's shipyard at Aberdeen of the *Scottish Maid*. According to the lines plan on page 59, the schooner measured 89.25 ft x 19.6ft (inside ceiling) x 11.4ft (approx) and 142 tons new measurement, and cost a total of £1700. The moulded breadth was 21ft. The sixty-four shares were divided between eighteen persons, of whom Alexander Nicol and George Munro were the managing owners with a joint holding of twelve shares, and many of the shareholders had an opinion to express on the design of the vessel, as described in this account from the *Aberdeen Journal* of 12 July 1848:

In the year 1839, a few spirited gentlemen in Aberdeen formed themselves into a copartnery, for the purpose of building a superior class of sailing vessels, to run in opposition to the steam-boats of the Aberdeen and London Steam Navigation Company. They applied to Messrs A Hall & Sons, shipbuilders, to construct a model for a fast schooner. The model was made as with the common bow, and orders were given to proceed with the vessel. The Messrs Hall commenced framing the schooner from aft, and continued the frames until they reached the fore end of the keel. Thus far the work had proceeded, when the builders suggested a deviation from the models, which they believed would prove to be a decided improvement. They proposed to run the stem out, so as to form the cut-water, the effect of which would be to draw the water lines finer at the bow, and, as a natural consequence, the vessel would divide the water easily, be more buoyant forward, and of less register tonnage, than if she were built on the old plan. The idea did not at first meet the views of the owners. A skeleton bow was then erected, and not a few of the curious examined it, and were sceptical of the uncommon design. After due consideration, the owners gave consent to proceed with the vessel according to the skeleton model, and in that style she was finished and launched. The look of the schooner in the water was encouraging. It was evident from the appearance of her water lines that the idea of a perfect bow was realized, and some of those who were first opposed to the project were now among its warmest commendators.

The new model necessarily implied a new style of masting and rigging. The sharpness of the bow, the fineness of the run, and breadth of the floor, suggested the importance of placing the masts so as to concentrate the force of the sails as much as possible on the centre of the vessel; and in order to increase her headway with a lively motion, it was deemed essential to give her spars a good rake aftwards.

Thus built and equipped, the *Scottish Maid* was put on the passage to London, and such were the qualities of her sailing that she frequently made the voyage in 49 hours. Encouraged by this result, the owners had other three clippers built on the same model, and so successful was the experiment, that 'clipper bows' became quite the rage, and the Messrs Hall had orders to construct vessels with the Aberdeen Bow, to trade in every part of the globe.

Up to the date of this article, thirty-six vessels had been built with the new bow and twenty-seven of them were schooners. As can be seen in the plans of the *Scottish Maid*, the knees and brackets of the headrails had been dispensed with, and the planking rabbet followed the line of the cutwater, giving a more streamlined appearance. Compared with many of the Baltimore clippers, the *Scottish Maid* was not that sharp, but she had power to carry sail and was evidently more fine-lined than the majority of the merchant brigs and schooners that were being built in the 1840's. Alexander Hall & Sons developed the form of their new hulls so as to effect a reduction of the tonnage calculated according to the new rule that became law in 1836, and when taken to extremes, the stem raked forward considerably and the sternpost aft, and the topsides tumbled-home before having a reverse outward curve up to the bulwarks. Tonnage by the new measurement (nm) rule then became less than by the old measurement (om) rule.

Shipbuilders at Dartmouth, Salcombe, Brixham, Shoreham and Ipswich, as well

Right: Lines plan of the schooner Rhoda Mary *drawn by the author from measurements taken off the vessel by Basil Greenhill and himself in 1949-51; at that time, she was an abandoned and derelict hulk on the River Medway and it may be that insufficient allowance was made in the plan for the apparent lack of sheer that had probably developed. Built on Restronguet Creek, near Truro, in 1868 of 118 tons net. The rudder, figurehead and keel below the rabbet have been reconstructed. Her longitudinal section and deck plan appears as fig 278 in the author's* Merchant Sailing Ships 1850-1875 *(1984).*

Page Opposite: Sail and rigging plan of the Rhoda Mary *reconstructed by the author to show her probable appearance when first built in 1868. It was assumed that when a mizen mast was added c1900 that the position of the mainmast was not altered, and that the main boom was cut in half. A painting of the vessel as a two-master corroborates most of the assumptions made.*

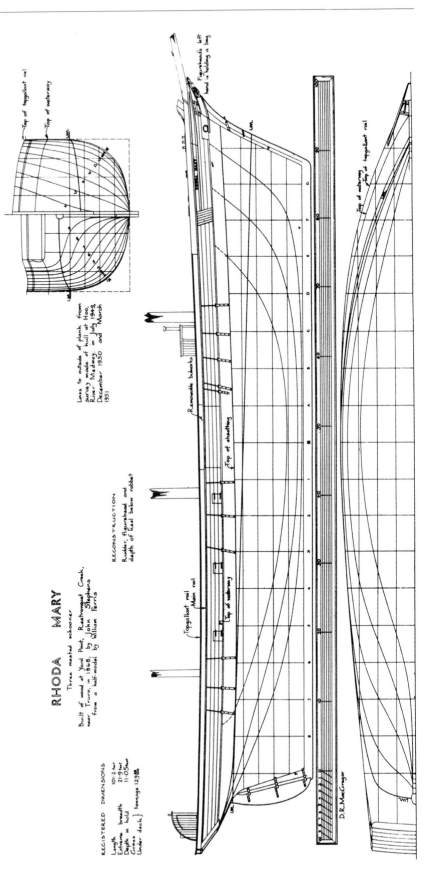

RHODA MARY

Three masted schooner

Built of wood at Yard Point, Restronguet Creek, near Truro, in 1868, by John Stephens from a half-model by William Ferris

REGISTERED DIMENSIONS

Length 101·2 feet
Extreme breadth 21·9 feet
Depth in hold 11·05 feet
Gross } tonnage 129·86
Under deck }

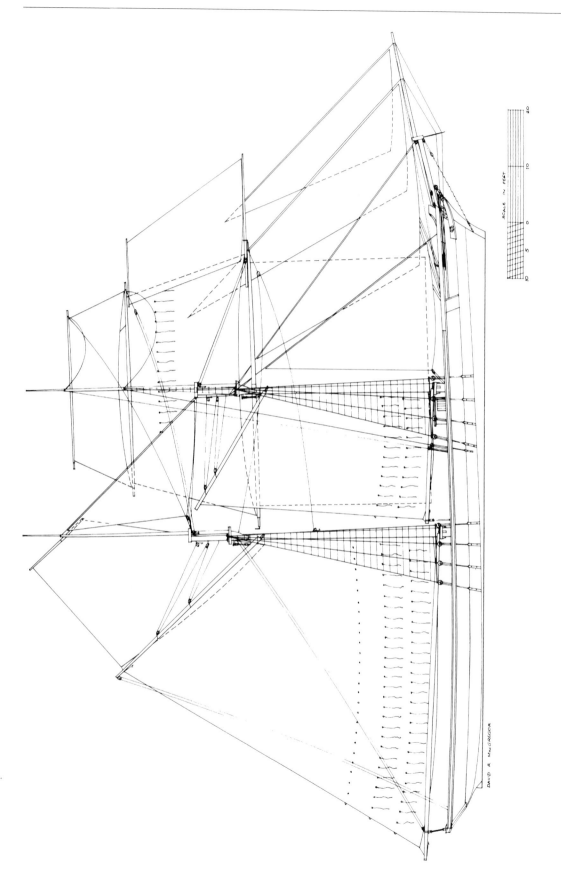

Opposite Calstock on the River Tamar c1895 can be seen James Goss's shipyard with the ketch Garlandstone *under construction. Lying alongside is the three-masted schooner said to be the* Rhoda Mary *and outside her the two-masted* Sunbeam. *Both schooners were built in the same year, 1868. (Courtesy Mark Myers, from the Michael Bouquet Collection)*

as at other ports, specialised in clipper schooners for the dried and fresh fruit trade, which was at its peak in the period 1840-70. Speed was all-important, and the sort of voyage time hoped for was the seventeen days' round-trip which the schooner *Elinor* took in 1869 from London Bridge to St Michaels in the Azores and back home again.

In his celebrated handbook entitled *On the Stowage of Ships and their Cargoes*, Robert W Stevens wrote in the 1869 edition under the section on 'Fruit':

Several schooners belonging to Brixham are built purposely for the Mediterranean trade; and are engaged almost entirely in it; they are long flat vessels with sharp ends, but much sharper aft than forward, so much so that little or no dunnage is required beyond the ballast, which is all placed in the narrow part of the hold. One of these schooners, the *Ocean Bride*, registers 144 tons, is 120ft overall, keel 92ft, extreme beam 22ft, and depth of hold 11ft 6in. She took in at Patras, in 1860, 180 ton (net) currants. The ballast, 20 ton, was all stowed abaft the main hatchway. With this cargo she was 8½ inches by the stern, in good trim; the upper part of the bends just awash. She will stow 50 ton of St Michael's oranges – 20 boxes to the ton – with 55 ton ballast.

The *Ocean Bride* cited here was built at Brixham by Richardson in 1859 and was owned in the same port by Sheers & Co.

The above quotation covers some of the design and stowage particulars of a typical clipper schooner of Devon or Cornwall. The reference to a 'flat vessel' probably means lack of sheer as exemplified in the lines plan of the schooner *Rhoda Mary*, whose hull Basil Greenhill and I first measured at Hoo in the River Medway in 1949. This schooner had a long sharp entrance and a long run with considerable hollow worked into the bottom half; the bilges were slack and the bottom started to round up close to the garboard strake. She measured 101.2ft x 21.9ft x 11.05ft and 118 tons net, and was built in 1868 in Restronguet Creek, off the western shore of the Truro River, by John Stephens. She is best known as one of the three fastest schooners in the British home trade, the others being the *Trevellas* and the *Katie Cluett*. She was a three-master for much of this century but began life with two

The Hope *was built at Bideford in 1849 and in her early days was in the fruit trade to the Mediterranean. When photographed here, the topgallant had been removed, double topsails had replaced her single sail, and studding sails had long since vanished.* (York Collection, Bristol Museum).

masts, and the sail plan on page 65 is an attempted reconstruction of what she might have looked like when new.

Some three-masters made their appearance in the 1850s, one of which was the narrow iron-hulled *Alma* which Gourlay Brothers of Dundee built in 1854 to sail to the Australian gold fields. At Shoreham, in Sussex, Henry Cheal Jnr records in *The Ships and Mariners of Shoreham* how James Balley launched the *Wild Dayrell* in 1856 of 310 tons, built with hollow waterlines and a 'Yankee three mast schooner rig'; but on her maiden passage 'she rolled away all her gaffs and booms' and had to put into Plymouth to refit. In the same year, Balley built the *Osprey* in the conventional style with four yards on her foremast at a cost of £3164. Due to the fact that so may harbours dried out at low water, British sharp-lined schooners could not afford to have much deadrise or else they were in danger of falling over on their sides when the tide ebbed. The design and construction of fine-lined schooners continued throughout much of the nineteenth century as there were always reasons why an owner wanted a fast vessel.

One fast deep-sea schooner was the *Susan Vittery* which was built at Dartmouth in 1859 by W Kelly, and after trading to the Azores and then carrying cod from Newfoundland, she had the distinction of being the last schooner in the British home trade to sail without an engine. Given a third mast in 1903 and renamed *Brooklands*, she survived the Second World War and was finally lost near the Tuskar in 1953 when sailing under her original name.

Stern view of the Brooklands, *ex-*Susan Vittery, *which was built at Dartmouth by W Kelly in 1859, and was originally in the fruit trade from the Azores. When sailing under her original name in the 1870s, her dimensions were given as 100.6ft x 21.4ft x 12.1ft and 140 tons net and gross. (Nautical Photo Agency)*

North American Schooners |

TWO- AND three-masted schooners are described in this chapter which concentrates on cargo-carrying vessels built in America with some reference to those built in the Maritime Provinces of Canada, leaving fishing schooners to be dealt with in Chapter 16. A good way to introduce this chapter is to quote from Henry Hall's *Report on the Ship-Building Industry of the United States*, written in 1882, in which he reviews the progress of the schooner rig:

> Another class of sailing vessel which grew into great repute before 1861 was the schooner. It has been noted that the original coaster was the sloop, its broad beam, shallow draught, big fore-and-aft sail and one or two jibs, simplicity of rigging and ease of management by about three men making it the right vessel for running along the coast and into and out of rivers. Ketches and brigantines were used for voyages as long as from Salem to Chesapeake Bay, for instance, and the two-mast-

This painting of the May *shows the sort of vessel used as a packet between Boston and New York or New Orleans in the 1830s. As the mizen is stepped so far aft it suggests that she might have been intended to be only a two-masted schooner. The foot of the square sail set from the fore yard is extended on a passaree boom. The* May *was of 126 tons and was built in 1833 at Essex, Massachusetts. (Courtesy of the Peabody Museum of Salem)*

ed schooner followed. During the packet times trade and travel increased so fast that large vessels were required for coasting, the square rig being preferred. Brigs, barks, and ships were much in favor, but after 1840 they went out of use for coasters, their places being taken on the one hand by steamboats, which were built for the passenger and mail service between all the large Atlantic and Gulf ports, and on the other hand by two- and three-masted schooners, built for freighting. The fore-and-aft rig came to be preferred for coasting vessels for several reasons. Fewer sailors were required to handle the vessel, and a schooner could be worked into and out of harbors and rivers more easily than any square-rigged craft. Her trips could also, as a rule, be made in quicker time, as she could sail closer into the wind, and it was hardly necessary for her to sail from Maine to New York by way of the

Purely fore-and-aft schooners were rare in Great Britain and in much of Northern Europe on commercial craft, whereas in the United States the reverse was the case after the 1850s, when square sails became a rare exception, particularly on the East Coast. Here the Mary Langdon *(built at Rockland, Maine, in 1845 and rebuilt in 1860 of 91 tons), presents a different profile to her British counterpart: she has two large deckhouses; a boat on the stern davits; a different-shaped stern; a wooden balustrade as far forward as the fore rigging because the deck was level with the main rail; 'lazy jacks' on the mainsail to prevent the sail spilling on to the deck when being lowered. These American schooners were broader in proportion to their length, the* Mary Langdon *having a length of 73ft which was equal to only 3.5 breadths.* (Courtesy of the Peabody Museum of Salem)

Bermudas, as some square-rigged vessels have done during baffling winds. The schooner rig became universal in the coasting trade about 1860, and there is probably not a bark or a ship left in this trade anywhere except on the Pacific coast, where the voyages are long and the winds blow in trades, and even there there are few purely square-rigged vessels in the trade. On the lakes the schooner is the popular rig, a few square topsails being sometimes added on the forward mast. Originally registering no more than 40 or 50 tons, the schooner has become in course of time a large vessel, the two masters ranging from 100 to 250 tons, the three-masters from 300 to 750 tons. The popular size now for a three-masted coasting schooner on the Atlantic is about 550 or 600 tons, and it is probable that more vessels of the schooner rig are built in the United States every year than there are of all other rigs put together. With square sails on the foremast the vessel is called a barkentine, and many of this class are used for transoceanic service, for which they are well adapted. The hulls of American schooners are as strongly built as those of any other vessels of their size; in fact, the scantling is far heavier than it was in full-rigged ships 75 years ago. They are constructed with a view to class A1 on the books of the American Shipmasters' Association, and no large ship can do better than that. The best materials and workmanship are put into them. For

In O S Lloyd's shipyard at Salisbury, Maryland, the three-masted schooner Hattie E Giles *(built 1874 of 135 tons) has had the planking stripped from her counter timbers. The davits for the stern boat are clearly shown. On the left is the two-master* Robin Hood *(built 1868 of 99 tons). Photograph taken c1903. (Courtesy of the Peabody Museum of Salem)*

Bowsprits and jibbooms of schooners projecting over the Miami waterfront. They had arrived laden with cargoes of timber for the first house-building boom of the mid-1920s. (Courtesy of the Mariners' Museum of Newport News)

transoceanic trade, and on the Pacific coast, where the waters are deep, the schooners are keel vessels with some dead rise; but on the Atlantic coast, where the harbors are so frequently shallow and obstructed with sand-bars, the schooners are center-board vessels with flat bottoms. In all cases, however, the models are full, the beam large, the bow sharp and long, the run clean, and the sheer considerable forward. Schooners with sharp bottoms do not pay, and few are built.

In the New England coasting business, fore-and-aft schooners of 50 to 75ft in length were preferred from about 1825, but topsail schooners and brigantines continued to be liked for trade to the West Indies or for taking cotton from the southern ports to New York. The biggest two-master in this trade was probably the *Langdon Gilmore* of 497 tons o.m. built in 1856 at Belleville, New Jersey. The coasting trade, by law, was confined exclusively to American vessels and so was highly protected with little chance of outside influences. The smaller two-masters often set no gaff topsail on the foremast and so a fore topmast was not required; of the two headsails, one hoisted on a stay from the bowsprit cap, and the other went to the end of the jibboom. The main gaff topsail was hooped to the topmast.

Three-masted schooners were not built much outside the Chesapeake area until the 1850s, but in that decade they suddenly became popular and forty-four vessels of 300 tons and upwards were constructed. In this same decade, the three-masters which had all their masts of equal height without any square canvas were known as 'tern schooners' or just 'terns', the word meaning three of a kind. Dividing the sail area into three gaff sails instead of two, resulted in narrower and lighter sails that were easier to handle; the spars could be shorter and therefore lighter and of smaller scantling, and the rigging not so heavy; there was also a possible crew reduction and noticeable lowering of costs. As schooners increased in size, a third mast was inevitable. Perhaps in the much wider bays and estuaries to be found on the Atlantic coast of America, compared with the British Isles, the absence of square topsails presented no problem to navigation, but in Great Britain some square canvas was considered essential in the narrower creeks and harbours, which were subject to much greater tidal changes. These tern schooners had the simplest of rigging and needed a smaller crew than those with those with square canvas; and although the gaff sails were really of similar size, the mizen sail was often larger than those on the other two masts. As regards their hull-form, some were of shallow draught with a centreboard, while others were much deeper and similar to a fore-and-aft rigged 'Downeaster'; but the most satisfactory ones were a compromise between the two, often including a centreboard.

Logs are being dragged out of the hold of this schooner through the gaping aperture of the bow port, and are then floated into the dock. This bow port had previously been used for loading a timber cargo into the hold, and the lid of the port was then locked into position and the seams caulked to make it watertight when at sea. The port lids – one each side – are hanging from tackles. This schooner is the three-masted Citnalta, ex-Esther Adelaide, *which was built at Fox River, Nova Scotia, in 1917, of 398 tons. She was rebuilt in 1936 and eventually foundered in 1942 in Long Island Sound after stranding.* (Courtesy of Mariners' Museum of Newport News)

Deck view looking aft aboard the three-masted schooner William Bisbee. *The broad wide decks, massive bulwark stanchions, and raised quarterdeck surrounding an after deckhouse are alien to British eyes but typical of American vessels. She was built in 1902 at Rockland, Maine, with a length of 133ft, a breadth of 31ft and 309 tons gross.* (Courtesy of W J Lewis Parker)

The first tern schooner to be seen in Great Britain was probably the *Eckford Webb* which sailed from Charleston to Queenstown in twenty-one days in 1855. There was an engraving of her in the *Illustrated London News* and an accompanying description:

This extraordinary craft recently arrived at Queenstown, where she has excited great interest from her remarkable performances. She is, in American nautical phraseology, 'tern-rigged', with three masts, each 84 feet long, on which are set three fore-and-aft mainsails; over these are set three gaff-topsails; she has also stay-sails in the main [and] mizen-topmast, but no square sails. Each mast is supplied with a splendid winch, by the aid of which two men hoist the sails in five minutes. She has in the log 309 miles for 24 hours; and the Captain (Graffam) states that during some of the hours she ran sixteen miles. She arrived from Charleston in twenty-one days, notwithstanding unfavourable weather during the passage. The *Eckford Webb* was built by Mr. Thomas Dunham, of New York. Her dimensions are –length, 137 feet; breadth, 30 feet. She carries 494 tons [this was incorrect; 494 tons was her register *not* her cargo capacity]; and her draught of water is 11 1/2 feet. Although loaded with 60 tons ballast, and 1560 square bales of cotton, she received orders from Messrs. N G Seymour & Co, and proceeded to the Baltic. She has only six men crew.

The lines plan of *Eckford Webb* was reconstructed by Howard I Chapelle and is reproduced in his book *Search for Speed under Sail* (plate XVI). She was a medium

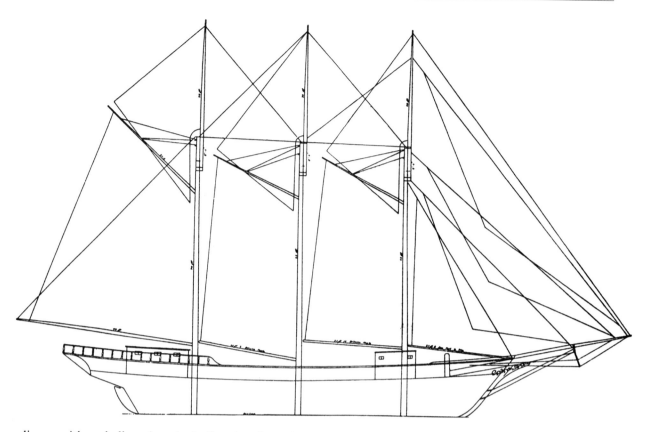

clipper with a shallow-draught hull and a short sharp entrance but a longer run; there was not much deadrise and the floors rounded up into slack bilges with marked tumblehome. On her return from the Baltic, Alexander Stephen & Sons hauled her out on their slip at Kelvinhaugh, Glasgow, where she remained for twelve days from 24 March 1856. That she excited considerable interest may be

This sail plan of the A V Conrad shows a typical tern schooner of the Maritime Provinces of Canada. She was built in 1908 at La Have, Nova Scotia, with dimensions of 101.6ft x 27.2ft x 10.0ft and 147 tons. The height of the mainmast from deck to truck was 91ft. This plan was traced by Dr Charles A Armour from the original and is reproduced through the courtesy of Everett Lohnes.

The tern schooner Nova Queen of 200 tons was built in Nova Scotia in 1919 and was lost with all hands in December 1924. Her deck is piled high with a timber cargo. (Nautical Photo Agency)

judged from the fact that I discovered her sail plan rolled up amongst other plans in Stephen's plan store during research work in 1961.

Larger schooners became increasingly necessary after 1850 to shift bulk cargoes of coal and lumber where good profits were to be made. The *Maritime Register* of New York commented on the situation in December 1881:

In late years nothing has been left for sail but coal and lumber and other coarse freights. Steam, however, some little time ago entered the coal trade also, and steam colliers have been steadily increasing in number to the great loss and injury of small coasting craft. Not only have the colliers taken away a large part of this

With rigging set up and sails bent, the tern schooner Edith M Green *of 189 tons is ready to be launched at Gilberts Cove, Nova Scotia, in 1917. (Courtesy of W J Lewis Parker)*

Photographed under a press of sail, Bill the Butcher *of 80 tons net was built at San Francisco in 1871*. (Courtesy of the Peabody Museum of Salem)

great trade, but at the loading point, the schooners have to give place to the more important steamer and wait until the latter is loaded before taking their turns at the coal wharf.

(Quoted also at greater length in Robert Miller, *The New York Coastwise Trade 1865-1915*.)

The abandonment of square topsails on most American schooners in the 1860s was a significant alteration in rig, but not content with this, a form of staysail rig was proposed by no less a man than Captain R B Forbes, who had introduced double topsails to America, and which was employed successfully in 1854 on the *R I Evans*, which made six voyages thus rigged to the West Indies. The lower four-sided staysails were fitted with deep bonnets which could be quickly unlaced to shorten sail; above these were other four-sided ones set on a stay from the topmast to the opposite mast head, just above the trestletrees; and the jib-headed topsails were set on

*The square-sterned schooner
Topaz lying beside a quay at
Chilton in the River Parrett
below Bridgwater. Built in
1860 in Prince Edward
Island, she was owned in
Wexford and was still afloat in
1910 when her ownership was
transferred to Mumford in the
Isles of Scilly; when first built,
she was of 96 tons, but by 1910
the various allowable
deductions had reduced her to
76 tons net.* (Photograph by
W A Sharman)

booms equivalent to conventional gaffs; this permitted all the sails to be operated
from the deck, without the men having to go aloft. But it was obviously not popular, partly because no innovation was ever liked, and partly because steam donkey
engines were being employed for hoisting the gaff sails.

A few scattered examples of vessels rigged as four-masted schooners appear
before 1880, although the first vessel built with four masts was, by all accounts, the
William L White, built in Bath, Maine, and quickly followed by many others.
Although it is the huge five- and six-masted schooners which have captured the
imagination, it should be remembered that the coastal waters were thronged with
small two- and three-masters of all kinds, and even brigs and brigantines were occasionally to be seen. With a skipper and crew of only two or three, sloops and
schooners kept expenses very low and by sailing close to the land they ensured a
supply of fresh food and an ability to keep in touch with home. One of the principal differences between British and American schooners was the after accommodation. American vessels had a large deckhouse aft which occupied almost the full
width of the deck space, and allowed only a narrow passageway each side on a level
with the poop, and reached by steps from the main deck; by contrast, British
schooners had their after accommodation situated below the main deck and
entered through a companionway and thence down steep stairs, thereby occupying
valuable cargo space. Originally the crew of an American schooner berthed forward

in a foc's'le below deck, as in British vessels, but in the mid-1870s, better accommodation was often demanded by American crews, especially in schooners trading with the West Indies, and this resulted in a foc's'le and galley being placed in a house built on the deck close abaft the foremast. In small vessels, the after deckhouse was often built large enough to house the crew at one end, as there was insufficient space for two deckhouses. Another contrast is afforded by the sheer size of an American three-masted schooner of 600-700 tons, in which all the hatchways,

On the Californian coast, about 100 miles north of San Francisco, is the Albion River and Alexander Findlay describes it in his Directory for the North Pacific Ocean *as being 'a very small stream, with the barest apology for a harbour at its mouth. A saw-mill upon this stream induces coasters to obtain freights here, but a great many of those trading have been lost.' It is in this situation that the three-masted schooner* Beulah *has been photographed loading timber, some of which has already been piled on her deck. A two-masted schooner with a big deck cargo lies ahead of her, ready to sail. The* Beulah *of 339 tons net was built at San Francisco in 1882 and in 1913 had a crew of seven. (Courtesy of the National Maritime Museum, San Francisco)*

mouldings, bulwarks, fife rails, windlass, deckhouses and so on have the sheer size and scantlings of a full-rigged ship, rather than those of the British schooner of 120 tons or less in which everything looks diminutive by comparison.

In the periodical publication *Log Chips* (editor and publisher John Lyman, Nov 1950 Vol II), there is an account of vessels built at Thomaston, Maine, by Samuel Watts, and of those listed between 1856-87, the first sixteen are all ships or barques; after that, from 1871, there are fourteen three-masted schooners, two four-masted schooners, and nine ships. As Watts was a master mariner, he employed a master carpenter or contract builders to construct the vessels which were launched under his name. John Lyman outlines the procedure in these words:

Samuel Watts owned a yard on the St George River at Thomaston, but at times, when building was brisk, would lease another site. The usual method of building

This is a view of San Francisco in November or December 1864 from Steamboat Point looking along South Beach. In the foreground are the modest buildings of a small shipyard with one schooner under construction and another ready for launching; in the Bay, eight two-masted schooners can be counted. (Courtesy of the National Maritime Museum, San Francisco)

*Under tow. From left to right
are the* Courtney Ford, *the
barquentine* Portland *and the
four-masted schooner* Eric.
*Standing at the stern of the tug,
in the centre, is Hiram Hudson
'Windy' Morrison.* (Courtesy
of the National Maritime
Museum, San Francisco;
Morrison Collection)

was for S Watts & Co to enter into a contract with the master builder to turn out a vessel of a given model and size, to class with Bureau Veritas, at a price agreed on per ton, builders' measurement, for hull and spars. Separate contracts were made with riggers, sailmakers, etc, and stores, boats, cabin furnishings, and sundry articles purchased to fit the vessel for sea. Meanwhile prospective part-owners were found, and the various shares to be distributed were agreed upon.

For someone not a shipwright by training, this arrangement ensured that a well-found schooner was built, and Samuel Watts would then take shares in her, the amount varying from one vessel to another.

An example of a small two-masted schooner of the 1860s was the *Mary Baker* of 101 tons, built in 1869 at Kingston, Massachusetts, which sailed for many years out of Boston and New York to the West Indies, but sometimes went fishing on the Grand Banks. Some of the Kingston fishing schooners were painted green both on deck and outside, but the *Mary Baker* had a black hull with a white strake above the waterway and a green bottom; bulwarks and deckhouse were painted white with blue mouldings, and the deck fittings were painted blue. Although the bowsprit was black, the jibboom, masts, gaffs and booms were varnished with white ends and doublings.

Howard I Chapelle published the lines and sail plan of the three-masted schooner *Marion F Sprague* in his monumental work, *History of American Sailing Ships*, describing her as 'an excellent example of [the] fine centerboard three-masted schooners of her period'. She was built in 1889 at East Boston with a length of 172ft 6in and a beam of 34ft 3in and 748 tons. She had a flat bottom, hard bilges, almost vertical sides, a convex entrance, a long concave run and considerable sheer. There was a raised quarter-deck which began between the fore and main masts, and instead of solid bulwarks there were turned wooden balusters with a rail capping. The caps of the lower masts were level and were joined by a triatic or 'jumper' stay. To enable the small crews to hoist the large gaff sails, it was common practice by this date to install a steam donkey boiler in schooners of this size and upwards for operating the capstans, halliard and cargo winches.

Concerning competition between sail and steam, Henry Hall in his *Report on the Ship-building Industry*, already referred to, reported one shipbuilder at Camden, Maine, as saying in 1882: 'A three-masted schooner of 600 tons will pay better for the amount invested than a steamer in the coal business. No one would think of carrying pitch-pine on a steamer.'

The first three-master recorded as built in Canada was the *Dispatch* in 1814 on Prince Edward Island, and several were built in later decades. The first tern schooner was the *Zebra* of 142 tons, built at La Have, Nova Scotia, in 1859. There were various boom times for building them and they enjoyed renewed popularity after the demise of the deep-water square-rigger. This was especially true during the first two decades of the twentieth century.

Many of the terns built in Nova Scotia in the First World War boom were designed on sharp lines, some being given a clipper bow and others a round bow similar to the fishing schooners. More than 150 of them were launched in 1918 and 1919. In *American Sailing Craft*, Howard I Chapelle gives the lines of the tern schooner *Marjory Mahaffy*, constructed in 1919 by John McLean & Sons at Mahone Bay, Nova Scotia, and the plan shows great deadrise with a long, convex entrance and a hollow run, with a deep drag aft. She was 130ft 3in long and had a reputation for speed, being heavily rigged with long gaffs. Schooners such as her brought salt from the West Indies and in turn took away salt fish to the Mediterranean, West Indies and South America. The last Nova-Scotian cargo-carrying schooner was reputed to be the *Mary B Brooks*, begun in 1920 but not completed until the year 1926.

Two-masted schooners were still being built on the Atlantic coast as late as 1914 and remained in use on the Maine coast, in Chesapeake Bay and the Gulf of Mexico carrying general cargoes, although lumber provided a regular trade to many vessels.

Three-masted schooners, some of them terns, continued to be built in varying sizes in every year with an especial boom in the period 1916-20. The last three-master, according to John Lyman, was the *Adams* built in 1929 at Essex, Massachusetts, and she measured 370 tons.

On the Pacific coast of America, shipbuilding activity was sparked off by the discovery of gold in 1849, and there was an immediate demand for small vessels to transport people and goods around the San Francisco Bay area and up the rivers. Of course, there were no shipyards in existence in the early days, but amongst those who had flocked there to make their fortunes were to be found shipwrights, amongst whom was John G North, a native of Norway, who opened a shipyard after only a few months of mining. In 1854 he constructed the three-masted schooner *Susan and Kate Deming*, which was no mean achievement, because by 1860 only about six vessels of over 100 tons each had been constructed in that area. Four two-masted schooners were built on the West Coast in 1861 and thereafter the numbers began to increase with every decade. The first three-master of over 300 tons was the *Sunshine*, built in 1875, and the first of over 400 tons was the *William Renton*, built in 1882. The first real four-masted schooners to be built on the West Coast appeared five years later, as will be told in more detail in Chapter 14. The last three-masted schooner, the auxiliary *Doris Crane*, was built in 1920. It is thanks to the researches of the late John Lyman that it is possible to write with certainty of such archival records.

Square topsails were carried for much longer on the Pacific coast than on the Atlantic coast, and four-masted schooners often carried a yard on the foremast to set a large square sail below. Another feature was to set a 'leg-of-mutton' sail on the aftermost mast instead of a gaff sail, together with a sort of topsail in the shape of a

The schooner on the left is a typical American West Coast lumber schooner named Lottie Bennett; *on her jigger mast is a leg-of-mutton sail and a 'ringtail' as a sort of topsail, both of which were regular features. She was built in 1899 at Port Blakely, Washington, and after twenty years in the lumber business she was sold for copra trading in the Pacific. The unidentified schooner on the right appears to have pole masts which are too short to set topsails, so she has resorted to a big four-sided staysail. (Courtesy of the National Maritime Museum, San Francisco)*

staysail hoisted from the boom end to the head of the topmast. This was locally called a 'ringtail'. The first authenticated case of this, wrote John Lyman, was the two-masted schooner *Rosario* in 1879. Even the big four- and five-masters used this rig.

Many of the later schooners had hulls which were designed to stand up without ballast and which were constructed with only one continuous deck, which was the main deck. This meant that in the 'tween decks there were a number of hold beams but no laid decks. Longitudinal strength was obtained by providing excessively deep keelsons and sister keelsons, and by bilge stringers which were worked into the ceiling.

Halfway through the first decade of the twentieth century, the construction of four-masted and three-masted schooners virtually ceased on the West Coast, but commenced again in 1916 in the middle of the First World War when a shipbuilding boom began. This was largely confined to schooners of over 1000 tons with four or five masts.

The barquentine rig was very popular on the West Coast even though the cost of the masts and yards on the foremast equalled the cost of all the other masts put together. The hulls usually had sharp ends and they could outsail the schooners; for long Pacific voyages the square canvas on one mast was ideal, and some schooners were converted to this rig.

A popular rig on the West Coast was the barquentine and its square canvas was ideal for long passages across the Pacific. This four-master is the Makaweli *of 899 tons which was built at Oakland in 1902; she was in the sugar trade to Hawaii.* (Kindly supplied by the late Robert Weinstein)

Victorian Schooners | *11*

IN THE twenty-odd years between the end of the Napoleonic Wars and the accession to the throne of the young Queen Victoria, the shape and appearance of the British schooner barely altered. Most were heavily rigged with a considerable amount of square canvas on the foremast which put many of them into the category of 'schooner brigantines' as described in Chapter 8. Some of these were built on fine lines but many were full-bodied and little different from coasting brigs or cutters in the packet service. A few open-decked boats, working in tidal rivers or estuaries, were schooner-rigged in these years according to the evidence of prints and paintings.

Remarkably enough, the sail plan of a merchant schooner, drawn to scale, was published in Edinburgh in 1830 by the naval architect, Peter Hedderwick, and from evidence in his book she can be identified as the *Glasgow* of 155 tons built in 1826. This sail plan together with her lines are reproduced in Chapter 6, from which it can be noticed that she has a small amount of deadrise, round bilges, a full

A misty morning looking towards the town of Falmouth with vessels lying head to wind. On the left is the deep-laden brigantine Frederike, *built at Papenburg in 1886, but no other vessels have been identified. Aboard the two-masted schooner in the right foreground, two of the crew are aloft on the topsail yard and another is on the topgallant yard. Other schooners lie ahead and to starboard.*
(MacGregor Collection)

An unforgettable sight in the harbour of Port St Mary, Isle of Man, as six schooners sit on the bottom in a few feet of water drying their sails in the light breeze. On the extreme left is the Margaret Garton, *built at the port in 1877 and of 52 tons, and directly astern of her and in the centre of the picture is another two-master, the* Venus *of Castletown, built at Perth in 1876 and of 72 tons. The others have not been identified.* (Courtesy of David Clement)

entrance and run, a square stern, a heavy head with trail boards, and a flush deck. This was the current style. The sail plan is very detailed but it should be noted that the rig is a variation on the normal topsail schooner rig. In this case, the *Glasgow* is rigged in a manner that was used quite extensively in northern Europe in which the topsail yard slid on the doubling of the fore topmast; above it was the topgallant which has greater depth than the topsail; and each of these two square sails has its own studdingsail. Possibly by 1840, the hull-form was becoming a little less box-like, particularly in the run, but the most notable change would have been the decrease in the depth of hold, due to the fact that a vessel's depth was actually being measured to calculate the tonnage. This amazing development became law in 1836, it having been assumed prior to this, by Act of Parliament, that the depth was merely half the breadth, and everyone took advantage of the fact. So hulls became shallower and therefore carried less cargo unless they were made longer, a proportion which increased their speed potential. Full-bodied hulls had required large sail areas to drive them along.

Schooners were becoming more popular after 1840 because they were cheaper to build and rig than brigs and required a smaller crew, and because of this there were smaller running expenses. Simultaneously, greater attention was being given to design – 'symmetry' was the popular word – and there was even a hint of finer-lined hulls, especially when competition with railways and steamers was concerned. How far the influence of clippers spilled into the building of everyday schooners is hard to assess, but they must undoubtedly have been discussed, particularly the ordering of the Aberdeen clipper schooner *White Mouse* by a Dartmouth shipowner from the yard of Alexander Hall & Sons at a cost of £1450 which is just over £20 per ton on 72 tons o.m. Great interest must have been evinced by local experts at finding an almost 'foreign' schooner competing in the fruit trade with the locally-built vessels.

Contemporary books on sailmaking and rigging give few direct references on how to tackle a schooner in about 1850, and they were still obsessed with a square-rigged foremast. The schooner-brigantine described in a previous chapter is still much in evidence in technical works, such as Robert Kipping's *Elements of Sailmaking* and George Biddlecombe's *Art of Rigging*, as well as Arthur Young's *Nautical Dictionary*.

Before the competition from steam became too intense, schooners were employed in the packet trade carrying passengers and light package goods between Scotland and the north of England to London, having supplanted the shorter, broad-beamed cutters which had all their sails on a single mast. Schooners were also employed on the Waterford to Bristol run, and likewise to the Channel Islands, from where they carried fresh vegetables and new potatoes to Southampton and London during the 1850s and 1860s.

Schooners were very busy in the fruit trade, and in *The Merchant Schooners* by Basil Greenhill are to be found some interesting statistics relating to it. In 1854 there

Three square-sterned topsail schooners crossing Mount's Bay, Cornwall, on the starboard tack. The vessel on the right is hoisting her upper topsail. (Courtesy of Frank E Gibson)

This three-masted schooner, the
Princess of Wales, was built
at Peterhead in 1863 by Stephen
& Forbes with dimensions of
100ft x 23ft x 11.4ft and 157
tons. An unusual piece of gear to
find in such a vessel is the
Cunningham roller-reefing
topsail, which is identifiable by
the sort of 'railway track' in the
sail. Other points of interest are
that the fore royal is furled, that
two of the headsails have reef
points, that the flying jib is
almost a storm sail, that the
mizen topmast is double – one
line passing to port and the
other to starboard of the
mainsail. As regards the deck
layout, there is a raised
quarterdeck; a sort of booby-
hatch painted white with a
pitched roof forward of the
foremost and another abaft the
mainmast; the usual galley,
longboat, after companionway
and skylight; a crew of six can be
counted. (Photograph made
from glass negative, courtesy
of the Peterhead Museum)

were seventy vessels involved in carrying the 60 million oranges and 15 million lemons which were exported from the Azores and western Mediterranean to London alone, and altogether 240 schooners were engaged in the trade. Pineapples were brought from the West Indies, melons came from Portugal, currants and other dried fruit were obtained from the eastern Mediterranean. Reference to some actual vessels in the trade was given in Chapter 9.

Two-masted and later three-masted schooners were in regular trade around the coastline of the British Isles and also to Europe and across the Atlantic, carrying cargoes from port to port in the 1860s and onwards into the twentieth century and right on into the 1920s. The introduction of the internal combustion engine, which was fitted to some vessels before 1914, heralded a change, but a few pure sailing vessels lingered on. Of the many cargoes carried, to name but a few, there was coal from north-east England, manure from London, China clay from Devon, slate from north Wales, iron ore from Cumberland (as it then was). The same schooners that were working coastwise might also pick up a charter for the Baltic to load timber, and if they were fortunate they might ship out a cargo to save going in ballast. There were also deep-water trades such as the carriage of salt cod from Newfoundland across the Atlantic to Spain, Portugal and Italy, or to South America; other schooners even made the long perilous voyage around Cape Horn to load copper ore in Chile.

An account of a rough passage in the schooner *Lancashire Lass* is recounted by George Sorrell in *The Man before the Mast*. This vessel was built in 1847 at Lancaster of 97 tons net and dimensions of 79.8ft x 18.2ft x 10.6ft, and when this experience occurred, she was owned in Sligo by Middleton & Co.

My fourth ship was named the *Lancashire Lass*, of Sligo, Ireland (from March 1861 to end of July 1862), schooner-rigged. In this vessel I stayed eighteen months, coasting between Liverpool, Sligo, Glasgow, Troon, Ardrossan, Killala, Ballina, Bristol, Gloucester, Garston, and Runcorn in the Mersey, also calling at a number of places – wind-bound – such as Lough Swilly, Belfast Lough, Lochandail, etc. [The last named is a wide bay on the south-west side of Islay, which is an island on the western side of Argyllshire, and the course to Sligo on the north-west coast of

SANDWICH.

To be SOLD by AUCTION

BY

MESS^{RS} HICKS & SON

On THURSDAY, 14th MAY, 1868,

(By order of the Mortgagee under a Power of Sale,)

THE

SCHOONER
"LADY BULLER,"

Of 50 TONS BURTHEN, N.M.,

TOGETHER WITH

Masts, Spars, Standing and Running Rigging, Patent Winch and Blocks,

70 FATHOMS of 7 in. TOW ROPE,

2 BOWER, 1 STREAM, & 1 KEDGE ANCHORS,

100 Fathoms ⅞ in. CHAIN CABLE, 14ft. BOAT, &c.

As she now lies ready for Sea, at WHARF ABOVE BRIDGE.

This handy Craft has been employed in the Corn Trade, and has just discharged a Cargo of Barley in excellent condition.

May be viewed on application to the AUCTIONEERS, *Market Street, Sandwich; and further Particulars had of* MESSRS. GRAY & Co., Solicitors, Whitby.

Sale at 2 o'clock in the Afternoon, at the Wharf.

E. F. GIRAUD, PRINTER AND STATIONER, 98, BEACH STREET, DEAL.

The Lady Buller, *advertised for sale at auction, was owned by William Sanderson at Whitby and was sold in 1868 to owners at Goole. She had been built at Salcombe in 1842, registered 50 tons, and her ownership at Whitby began in 1850. This is a typical poster, although sometimes there is a brief inventory of sails and gear at the bottom. In a few cases, there is also, on the reverse side, a detailed inventory of all the vessel's stores, fittings, gear and even cutlery. (MacGregor Collection)*

A stern view of the topgallant yard schooner Lord Devon *on the foreshore at Salcombe. She was built there in 1885 of 98 tons and was copper sheathed.* (Fairweather Collection, by courtesy of Malcolm Darch)

The steel-hulled C & F Nurse, *photographed under full sail with her yards braced sharp up, and heeling over in a fresh breeze on the starboard tack. She was built at Falmouth in 1900 by William H Lean for the Nurse family of Bridgwater.* (Courtesy of David Clement)

Having been built on the open beach beneath the high cliffs at St Agnes, the Trevellas *was photographed ready for launching in 1876. The builder was M T Hitchins and she measured 97.0ft x 22.3ft x 11.4ft and 121 tons net. She had a reputation as a fast sailer.* (Richard Gillis Collection)

The three-masted schooner
Silvia *under sail in a fresh
breeze. This is almost certainly
the vessel built at Appledore of
164 tons in 1871 by William
Pickard, because the only other
schooner of this name in*
Lloyd's Register *was a
French vessel spelled* Sylvia
(1869). The Silvia *began life
as a two-master owned at
Hull, but she had a third mast
added by 1896. In this
photograph, the gaff jaws of the
foresail are well below the
hounds because a reef has been
taken in the sail. The mizen
has also been reefed.*
(MacGregor Collection)

Ireland would take a vessel out into the open Atlantic. The head of the Bay is about 12 miles from the open sea. Sometimes now spelled Loch Indaal.] On one occasion, when coming out of the last named bay into the Atlantic, we had a very narrow escape. We were from Liverpool and had passed through the North Channel on our way to Sligo, when on account of the very heavy head weather we up helm and ran for Lochandail, and remained there for some days, when the weather moderating and the wind veering we got under way. The fleet consisted of about eighteen vessels, large and small, and it so happened that we were the last to trip anchor, and by the time sail was all set we observed some of the vessels returning and shortening sail, as the already stiff breeze began to freshen in earnest. We, however, held our course, and the whole fleet passed us on their return to anchorage, not caring to face the very heavy seas to be seen in the offing.

Only one small sail was taken off as we neared the lighthouse, and as we passed from under the shelter of the land into the broad Atlantic we found ourselves in the water; this was caused by the heavy press of canvas that we carried, and meeting all at once those western rollers. The only way I can account for the *Lass* recovering herself again was that the water failed to get below, every opening having been securely battened down, for from experience we knew that the *Lancashire Lass* was fond of the water. During this time we were clinging to the rigging, endeavouring to do what ought to have been done before – that is, to get some of the sail off; but there was only one way that it could be done now, and that was by the knife. Several of the crew called out, 'She is sinking!' and, in fact, I thought so too; one heavy sea dashed straight through the jibs, and with the wind carrying away some of the other sails, with the help of the knife – for it was impossible to get under water to let go the ropes in the ordinary way – the vessel recovered herself somewhat. Not until then had we a moment's breathing time to look around and pay some attention to the hull. We found all the lee bulwarks had disappeared, the boat was smashed, and all loose articles gone.

The schooner reached Sligo a few days later in time to celebrate New Year's Day 1862. George Sorrell later bemoans the fact that he had to lie down to sleep in his oilskins because of water coming through the seams in the deck planking and adds that dry planking would have been a luxury to rest on. The *Lancashire Lass* went missing at the end of the 1860s, but another schooner of the same name had been built in 1863.

The rise and fall of the tide had a strong influence on the design of schooners, because unless they could remain constantly afloat they required the ability to sit moderately upright on the bottom at low water as the tide ebbed away. In the Baltic, the Mediterranean, American ports south of Boston and in equatorial zones, the rise and fall of the tide was small or negligible, and vessels with steep deadrise could remain permanently afloat. In Great Britain, northern Europe and the Maritime Provinces of Canada, vessels had to take the ground twice a day unless they could lie in one of the few docks with lock gates. At most harbours in the British Isles, brigs and brigantines, schooners, ketches, smacks and barges could be seen at low water in various ungainly positions, and woe betide the skipper or mate who had not taken the right precautions. A craft with steep deadrise, unless secured beside a quay, would just lie on her side and might not rise as the tide flooded.

William Trebilcock remembered how, in the trading smack *Mary*, they were lying at Penryn loading cargo from the schooner *Millom Castle*. As the tide rose, so did the *Mary*, but the half-empty *Millom Castle* did not. Only when the water was within a foot of her deck did she suddenly rise out of the water like a whale, breaking the suction of the Penryn mud, with her masts shaking and the rigging slatting to-and-fro. Expecting trouble, a crew sometimes passed chains around the hull which could be hauled up and down to break the suction.

Therefore schooners had to be built without too much deadrise but they could have sharp ends to achieve speed. There were really

Most of the schooners and ketches continued to use deadeyes and lanyards instead of rigging screws for setting up their rigging, and here at Appledore, two men from the yard of P K Harris & Sons are attending to the main rigging of the ketch Democrat *in June 1951.* (Author)

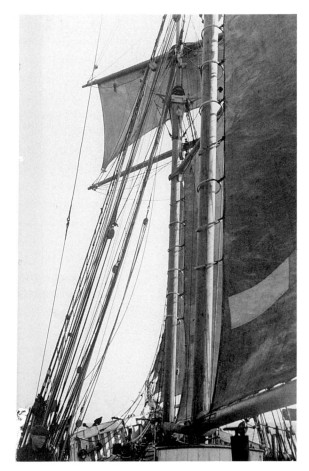

Above: Aboard the two-masted schooner Katie *which was one of the last sailing vessels in the United Kingdom trading under sail without an auxiliary engine. Photographed by Michael R Bouquet in the winter of 1939-40, looking down on the after deck from the foremast. The* Katie *was built at Padstow in 1881 and in 1940 her dimensions were given as 88.5ft x 23.0ft x 10.8ft and 96 tons net. (Courtesy of Mark Myers from Michael Bouquet Collection)*

Above right: Aboard Katie, *looking forward with a square lower topsail set in 1939-40. Dick Brenton, the cook, is in the left foreground. Note the galley chimney on right, which was used at sea to avoid the main boom. Photograph by Michael Bouquet. (Courtesy of Mark Myers from Michael Bouquet Collection)*

two basic forms of hull in the second half of the nineteenth century: one was put into fast-sailing craft and consisted of a long convex entrance with almost vertical bow sections, together with a long and concave run; the other, normally intended for vessels where cargo capacity was the prime consideration, had more balanced ends, possibly even with hollows in the fore-body but certainly hollow aft. The first type of hull-form can be seen in the plans of the *Rhoda Mary* reproduced on page 64 and the other style can be viewed in plans of the *Millom Castle* on page 97.

Deck layouts did not vary much from one schooner to another, although they differed endlessly in detail. In a two-masted schooner, the windlass for heaving in the anchor had a wooden barrel and an 'Armstrong patent' apparatus for revolving it, and it was situated at the fore end of the deck, either right in the bows or at the break of the foc's'le. The scuttle to the crew's quarters below deck was close abaft the windlass. Next came the fore hatch, followed by the foremast, galley, main hatch – on top of which lay the longboat in chocks; then came the mainmast, pumps and fife rail, after hatch, skylight to the cabin, companion to the after accommodation for the master and mates, and finally the binnacle and wheel. In a three-masted schooner, the mizen would be stepped between the after hatch and the cabin skylight. All the above items were basic requirements in brigs, brigantines and barquentines, and so similar deck layouts were to be found in most types of vessels.

Above: Another photograph by Michael Bouquet aboard the Katie; *looking down on the fore deck when beating up the River Thames in the spring of 1940. There are four headsails set. (Courtesy of Mark Myers from Michael Bouquet Collection)*

ALL SAILS STORED AT OWNER'S RISK

H. S. PRIOR,

SAIL MAKER.

AWNING, BLIND & COVER MAKER.

PHONE : 705.

CHURCH STREET,

FALMOUTH.

(At rear National & Provincial Bank)

Flying Jib 67 yds
Boom Foresail 166 yds
Fore Staysail 84 yds
Squarsail 98 yds.
Mainsail 212 yds Twine
Standy Jib 54 y a Twine
Boom Jib 66 yds Twine
Gaff Topsail. 80 to 90 yds

about Sizes for

Katie Schooner

1,000
7/6

Above: List of sail areas for the two-masted schooner Katie, *probably prepared about 1930. The dimensions will be 'running' yards of canvas, 21in wide, and not areas. (MacGregor Collection)*

Left: A closer view of the cargo winch, windlass and in-board portion of bowsprit aboard the Katie; *note the fore staysail set on a boom. Photographed at Deptford by H Oliver Hill in June 1939, who loaned me his negative.*

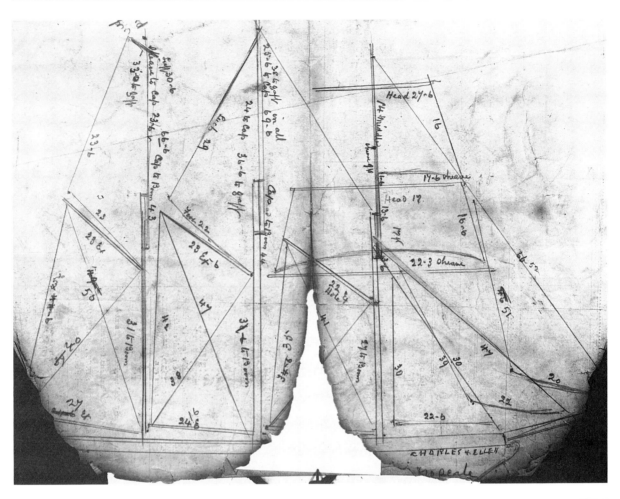

Above: A sail plan of the Charles & Ellen *drawn on the back of a Falmouth poster bearing the date of 6 January 1916, and found in Penrose's sail loft, who were successors to Prior & Holdroff. This schooner dropped out of the* Mercantile Navy List *between 1917 and 1919. She had been built of iron at Barrow in 1878 by D Noble & Co, and had only two masts when launched. Length was 106.2ft and she measured 145 tons. (MacGregor Collection)*

Right: The author digging a trench through the mud and debris on the inside of the Millom Castle *in order to take offsets. Photographed by Ralph Bird using the author's camera.*

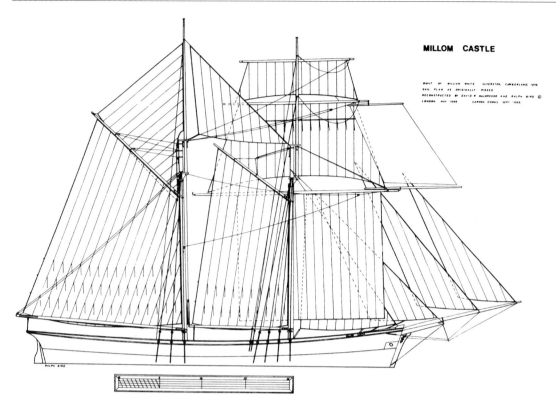

MILLOM CASTLE

Sail and rigging plan of the Millom Castle *drawn and reconstructed by Ralph Bird with suggestions by the author. No list of spar dimensions existed. Sources: painting by R Chappell, photographs of vessel, sail plans of contemporary schooners, books on mast-making and sailmaking.*

Lines plan of the two-masted schooner Millom Castle *drawn by Ralph Bird from lines taken off vessel to inside of ceiling by him and the author in October 1978. She was built at Ulverstone, Cumberland, in 1870 of 84 tons net. Reconstruction: bulwarks at stern, rudder, outside form of hull below bilge, load waterline, shape of forefoot.*

MILLOM CASTLE

Built in 1870 at Ulverston, Cumberland by William
White for William Postlethwaite of Millom, Cumberland
Reg. dimensions:

Length	—	81.2
Beam	—	20.6
Depth of hold	—	9.5
Reg tons	—	78
Rig	—	Schooner

Found derelict in a creek on the River Lynher, Plymouth
by David R MacGregor in 1960.
Lines taken off in October 1978 by David R MacGregor
and Ralph Bird.
Further dimensions taken off in December 1978 and July
1979.

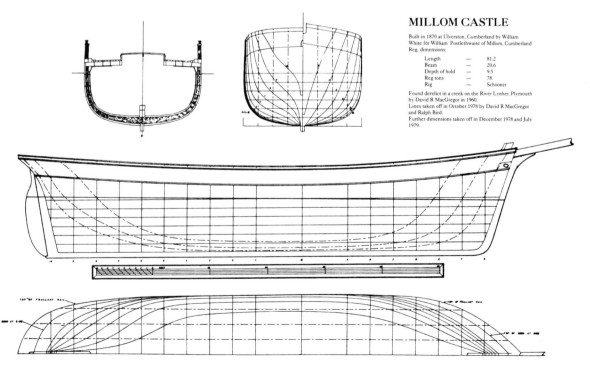

On the quayside at Charlestown, Cornwall, men are standing in horse-drawn carts and shovelling china clay down chutes into the hold of the two-masted schooner John Farley. She was constructed at Bideford by John Johnson in 1864 with dimensions of 82.0ft x 20.0ft x 10.7ft, 108 tons and classed 12 A1. In this narrow wet dock, there was space for three vessels abreast; the vessel in the centre has not been identified, although the port of Liverpool can be read on the wheel cover; the schooner on the far right is the Henry Edmonds, which was built at Aarhus, Denmark, in 1871. Astern of the John Farley are lock gates into the tidal outer basin. (Photograph provided by Peter Ferguson from a copy negative in the Terry Belt Collection)

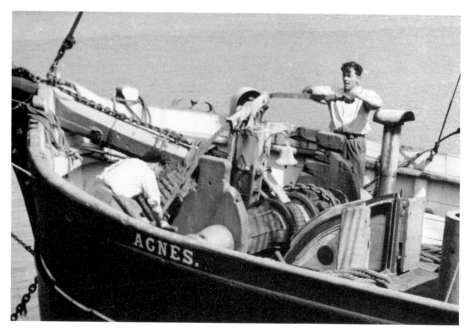

Two of the crew of the ketch
Agnes, *at Appledore in the
early 1950s, are working the
up-and-down handles on the
'Armstrong' patent windlass to
heave in the anchor chain. This
back-breaking task forced the
apparatus to revolve the
wooden barrel as had been
performed for the previous
century in countless schooners,
brigs and larger square-riggers.*
(Author)

The wooden planking of the decks was sometimes holystoned to a light creamy colour but many schooners painted their's red or blue. Bulwarks were frequently white inside with mouldings and rail picked out in a colour. Masts, yards, gaffs and booms were often varnished, and the masts from deck level to height of the boom saddle were often red, blue or green to match the deck fittings. The galley, companion and other wooden fittings were either varnished or painted or a combination of the two. Externally, hulls were almost invariably black with a white or gold band at the sheer strake which continued up to the top edge of the trail board carving; sometimes the bulwark rail was also white. A good way to tell if a schooner was going 'foreign' would be the copper sheathing on her bottom below the load water-line, designated in *Lloyd's Register* by the letters 'Y M'. An external colour scheme of 'painted ports' on the hull was rare and then only on the longer schooners.

Schooners in Europe, both British and Continental, almost invariably carried square sails on the foremast so that the term 'schooner' automatically assumes this fact; indeed, if square sails were absent, the term 'fore-and-aft schooner' had to be employed to mark the difference. Conversely in America, a schooner was automatically deemed to be fore-and-aft rigged and so the presence of square canvas on the foremast drew the term 'topsail schooner'. Sometimes, schooners in Europe which crossed a topgallant yard were called 'topgallant yard schooners'.

Although the square sails were regularly set, the gaff sails formed the largest areas of canvas. Single topsails were usually not replaced by double ones until the 1880s at which time older vessels often did away with the topgallant and shortened the height of the topmast. A square sail was often set below the fore lower yard in favourable winds, although it was often cut to set only on the weather side of the yard. Of other fore-and-aft canvas, four headsails were usually carried with a main topmast staysail; in addition there was a jib-headed topsail on the mainmast or, in earlier vessels, one with a head yard. Studdingsails were regularly set outside all the square sails until the end of the 1870s and some captains continued their use

Above: With canvas reduced to foresail and one headsail, and with the help of her engine, the Isabella *makes her way into Newlyn harbour. This schooner with her 'Irish Sea stern' was built at Barrow by Ashburner in 1878 of 75 tons; this is the type of stern to be seen on* Millom Castle. *This* Isabella *should not be confused with another schooner of similar name which was built near Dartmouth in 1864.* (John Munn)

Right: An unidentified three-masted schooner under sail, probably returning from an ocean voyage, is bartering with a tug that has ranged alongside her off Bootle for the cost of being towed into the River Mersey. Not many sails have been taken in yet, although the fore staysail is being hauled down. (Basil Lavis Collection)

until the end of the century; indeed the booms were photographed on the *William Morton* as she was towed up the River Avon to Bristol in 1915.

In the second half of the nineteenth century, some schooners were built with round sterns but the majority had square ones with the traditional wing transom. However, there was a form of round stern that could have developed from eighteenth century hull-forms and which was colloquially called the 'Irish Sea stern' because it was mostly found on craft built in shipyards bordering this sea. Such a hull was double-ended with the rudder head outside the hull, and the entire stern was framed with cant timbers, as at the bow, thus removing the need for overhanging counter timbers and transoms. It resulted in a very strong structure. The Dutch had found it successful in the flutes, and some of the billy-boys in the North Sea also used it. Or it could have developed from the 'galliot' which was used in north-west England and which was described in Arthur Young's *Nautical Dictionary* of 1846 as 'a flat-bottomed vessel whose bow and stern are similar, being round and bluff . . .'. Appledore men disparagingly called them 'Barrow flats', but they had several advantages: they were of shallow draught, they sailed on an almost even keel, were good sea boats, could sail without ballast, were cheap to build and immensely strong.

Possibly the only surviving example was the *Millom Castle* which was lying deeply embedded in the mud of the Lynher River. I found the hulk in August 1960 but there was no name on her. However, I made a note of her official number which was carved into the main beam in the correct manner, and passed the information on to Cmdr H Oliver Hill, who was able to identify her. Before she disintegrated too much, Ralph Bird and I were able to take off her lines and he has reconstructed a fine plan (page 97) which shows a full-bodied vessel with full ends, slight deadrise with slack, rounded bilges and some 20ft of dead flats amidships. The splendid quality of her pitch pine planking, both externally and internally in the ceiling, had held her together, and

there were few butt joints to be found. According to the Lloyd's Register survey report, the keelson and rider keelson, both of pitch pine, had no scarphs and so were presumably in one piece each from stem to stern. The frames were of oak; nearly all the sixteen deck beams were of larch and the deck planking was yellow pine. She was classed 10 A1 in *Lloyd's Register* and was of 91 tons with a length of 81.2ft and a beam of 20.6ft. Forming one of the fleet of twenty-eight vessels owned in the 1870's by William Postlethwaite of Barrow, she was designed to carry cargoes of iron ore and coal from the Cumberland and Lancashire mines. Ralph Bird has reconstructed a sail plan to show how she might have looked when launched from the shipyard of William White at Ulverston in 1870.

No attempt has been made to describe any of the many disasters that took place on a daily basis, but scanning the pages of the shipping papers in the nineteenth century one cannot help but notice the continual reporting of wrecks, strandings, collisions and vessels posted missing, both at home and abroad. An example of a schooner going ashore in a gale near Bude is a typical example, as reported in *Bencoolen to Capricorno*, which is a book describing wrecks at Bude from 1862-1900.

The three-masted schooner Bessie *of Salcombe photographed in Dover Harbour in the 1880s after a collision, which has removed her bowsprit and partly wrenched off her cutwater. She had been built at Kingsbridge in 1871. Note the iron cathead with dog standing on the in-board end.* (Richard Gillis Collection)

Unloading cargo from the three-masted schooner Mary Barrow *into a cart at Custom House Quay, Falmouth. The fitting of the figurehead, the mouldings, the patterned trail boards, the chain rigging – in fact, the whole assembly of the bows – is well illustrated here. A deck scene taken aboard her when under sail appears on page 112.* (MacGregor Collection)

December 22, 1894. The following account is, I believe, from the *Western Morning News* of December 24th, 1894, but the cutting kindly lent to me only bears a pencil date. 'Shortly after noon, a schooner in a disabled condition, and with a flag of distress flying, was sighted in the bay, apparently making for Bude. Her captain, apparently, was unable to do this, and then headed his vessel for Widemouth Beach, a long stretch of sandy shore, with rocks above and below, about 2½ miles west of Bude, where the ill-fated craft struck between four and five in the afternoon. Tremendous seas washed over her as she neared the shore, and, with the exception of the two at the wheel, the crew took to the rigging, her captain giving instructions from aloft. The great wonder is, how anyone could have remained on board at such a fearful time. She proved to be the *Elter Water*, Doyle, master, belonging to Arklow, and bound from Swansea to Cherbourg, with a cargo of coal and patent fuel. She sailed on Thursday, and when off Godrevety, on the Cornish coast, encountered the late heavy gale, first from the south-west, and then from the north-west, with thick weather and rain. The ship was then put about, and bore away up the Bristol Channel. She was about 230 tons burthen, and 90 register, and appears to have lately undergone expensive repairs.

The Bude Coastguard and Brigade were promptly at the scene of the wreck, and

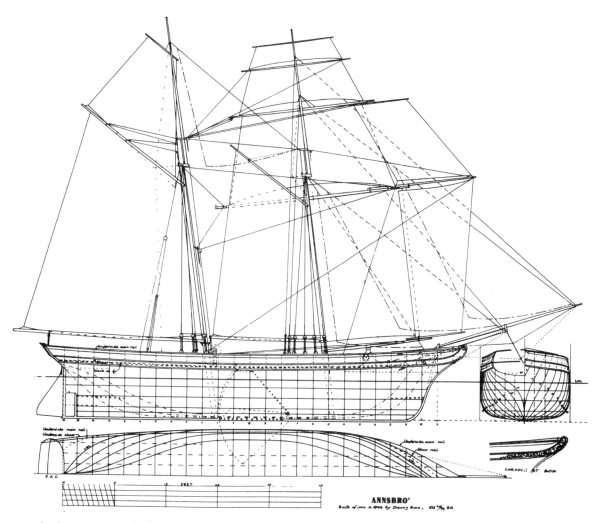

ANNSBRO'
built of iron in 1846 by Denny Bros., 105 ³⁄₄ tons

worked most energetically at the rescue, although beset with several difficulties from lines fouling on shore, and other obstructions on board the vessel. The rescue was not effected until between eight and nine in the evening, and then not until one of the coastguard very pluckily volunteered to be sent out in the breeches to ascertain the nature of the obstruction, which prevented the crew coming ashore by means of the apparatus. The whole scene was weird in the extreme, one not to be easily forgotten, and which appeared to be for some time a veritable struggle between life and death; for, as the tide would soon begin to make, the position of the crew was becoming more and more perilous. The position was wild and exposed, the sea heavy, the subsiding gale bitterly cold, and the darkness greatly added to the difficulty of the work of the rescuers. The names of the crew saved by the rocket apparatus taken from Bude are: Doyle, master; Tracey, mate; Nail, Kelley, and Price, all seamen belonging to Arklow.

The ship did not ebb dry, and it was highly necessary to get the crew ashore before the tide commenced to flow.'

The reporter became quite lyrical in describing the schooner in the grip of the breakers but failed to give any description of the working of the breeches apparatus.

Lines and sail plan of the Annsbro' *drawn and reconstructed by F A Claydon from two plans at the National Maritime Museum, Greenwich. Built of iron in 1846 by William Denny at Dumbarton of 105 tons. It was uncommon for the builder to draw studding sails and their rigging on his own sail plan. Principal reconstruction: jibboom outside cap, dolphin striker and rigging to it, all headsails and main topmast staysail, deadeyes and lanyards. Triangular centreplate omitted in favour of the one drawn here. Note aperture for screw propeller.*

Right: Two schooners drying their sails at low water at Newlyn. On the left is the three-master Jasper, *built at Falmouth in 1884 and wrecked in 1904; she was of 129 tons net and her length was 96ft. On the right is the smaller* Amanda, *built at Padstow in 1867 of 87 tons and a length of 82.7ft; two of her crew are working aloft on the topsail yard. The seams in her gaff sails are unusually prominent.* (Courtesy of David Clement)

Below: A melancholy end to the Susan Elizabeth *at St Ives. She had been built as a cutter at Salcombe in 1857, but was re-built ten years later when she was presumably re-rigged as a schooner; she was then of 70 tons.* (Courtesy of Frank E Gibson)

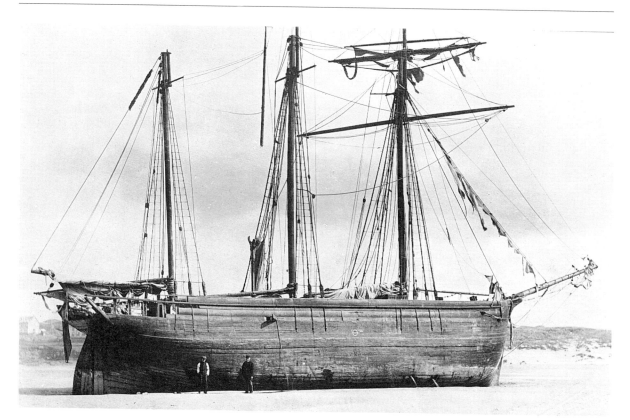

The *Elter Water* was built at Maryport in 1857 and measured 80.0ft x 20.3ft x 12.3ft and 100 tons net register; she was a wooden two-masted schooner and had been given a new keelson in 1876.

Not many schooners were built of iron because it required a shipyard with reasonably sophisticated equipment for cutting and bending the frames and plates, as well as the services of a draughtsman to make plans, and such yards usually concentrated on larger sailing vessels and on steamers. However, two such yards on the Clyde, Alexander Stephen & Sons and Denny Bros, built a few schooners for which plans have survived. Stephen's built the two-masted schooner *Angelita* in 1859 with a length of 100ft and of 129 tons; she had a deep narrow hull with a proportion of six beams to length and could equally well have been rigged as a brig. She 'careened in launching' noted Alexander Stephen in his diary, probably meaning that she fell over on her side as she went down the ways. She was built for the copper ore trade with Chile, which necessitated rounding Cape Horn.

Alexander Stephen also built a three-masted schooner named *Metero* for the copper ore trade; she was of composite construction and was launched in 1866 with dimensions of 120ft x 26ft x 9ft and 191 tons register. These dimensions gave her a broad beam and shallow draught which was a strange hull-form to send around Cape Horn, and possibly the fact that she stranded off Valparaiso on her maiden passage indicates that she possessed insufficient weatherly qualities. One would have expected a centreboard for such a hull-form, but they were rarely fitted in Great Britain because regularly having to take the ground in harbours which dried out, caused them to get jammed with debris.

However, Denny Bros built an iron schooner with a big centreboard pivoting on

The three-masted schooner Enterprize *got into difficulties in a severe gale in September 1903, and the St Ives lifeboat took off the crew of four and allowed the vessel to drift. Eventually she grounded on the Western Spits, half-a-mile west of Hayle Bar. She was an old vessel, having been built at Newport in 1846, with a length of 87.3ft and of 93 tons net. She was carrying 118 tons of China clay. The schooner in this photograph was identified by Terry Belt.* (Courtesy of Frank E Gibson)

On deck beside the mizen mast, two men, presumably the master, Hugh Evans, and the mate, survey the wreckage of their schooner, the Enterprize, *after she had driven further up the beach. With the crew, they had gone aboard to collect their possessions. The owner in Beaumaris sold the vessel by auction for £11, and she remained there until broken up by heavy seas in February 1904. Data on the wreck from Richard Larne's* Shipwreck Index of the British Isles. *(Courtesy of Frank E Gibson)*

the keelson. This was the *Annsbro'* of 105 tons built in 1846 and her lines plan, combined with the sail plan, is shown on page 103. She is flat-floored with sharp ends and is heavily rigged with a fore royal above her topgallant; the builder's sail plan has a topmast and a lower studdingsail drawn. Here are two examples of centreboards being removed: when the iron sloop *Clipper* (1844) was re-rigged as a schooner in 1847, her 'sliding keel' was removed; in 1857, the three-masted schooner *Phantom* of 210 tons, built four years earlier in New York by George Steers, had her's removed at Appledore.

Unlike the United States, the size of schooners did not increase dramatically in the United Kingdom as the century wore on, and the only noticeable alteration was the insertion of a third mast. The word 'insertion' is used deliberately as many two-masters reduced their extremely long main booms by half, and added a mizen mast. Frequently the mainmast did not have to be shifted. Simultaneously, the fore topgallant was discarded and the single topsail replaced by double ones on a shortened fore topmast; the studdingsail booms would also be removed at such time, if they had not been unrigged earlier. As regards the design of schooners towards the end of the nineteenth century, the general hull-form did not alter much except that hulls were longer and fuller-bodied amidships, although few were built with any real parallel middle body.

However, in the North Atlantic trade there was room for improvement and a breed of fine two-masted and three-masted schooners was developed which earned respect and admiration. The export of salt cod from Labrador and Newfoundland was an ancient one and due to the smallness of many of the settlements at which the fish was cleaned, salted and laid out to dry, only small vessels could be employed.

In the 1860s, fruit schooners were being chartered for Atlantic voyages from Brixham and Salcombe. It was a hard slog to windward and the Toast 'Forty days to the Westward!' epitomised the hard-driving masters intent on making a fast passage. Many vessels took months to sail across and only the finest schooners were employed. By contrast, once loaded, they sped before the westerlies bound for European ports and frequently made the crossing in less than twenty days, several taking under two weeks. Some schooners made only one or two round trips per year but others built specifically for the trade were sailing continuously back and forth, even in winter. This was a really hard life both for the crew and for the vessel.

The principal ports from which the schooners sailed were Portmadoc and Fowey, and the trade was at its height in the years 1880 to 1910. John Stephens of Fowey owned a large fleet in the trade, many rigged as schooners, of which he was very proud. In 1895 his *Spinaway* took fifteen days between St John's and Oporto; a year later the *Little Secret* sailed from Trinidad to Gibraltar in seventeen days. Perhaps it

An unidentified barquentine driven ashore on a Cornish beach appears to be badly damaged. Horses and carts are going down to off-load cargo and other gear from the stranded vessel. When there was no port to enter, ketches, schooners and brigs often unloaded their cargo into waiting carts on the beach in a similar fashion to this scene, perhaps taking more than one tide to do so. (MacGregor Collection)

Charter-Party.   Ardrossan, *30th July* 1891

R. L. ALPINE & Co.,

Coal Exporters, Timber Importers,

SHIP & COMMISSION AGENTS,

ARDROSSAN.

TELEGRAPHIC ADDRESS:
"ALPINE, ARDROSSAN."

IT IS THIS DAY MUTUALLY AGREED BETWEEN *Captain Jones*

of the good ~~Sailing~~ Ship or Vessel called the "*Annie Crossfield*" of *Barrow*

measuring *95* register tons, or thereabouts, now *here*

and *R. L. Alpine Co* of *Ardrossan* Merchant s

That the said ~~Sailing~~ Ship being tight, staunch, and strong, and every way fitted for the voyage,

shall proceed to *a loading berth* and there load a full and complete cargo of

Coals say *190* tons, or thereabouts (the Captain to take on board sufficient Coal

for Ship's use, to be kept separate from Cargo and endorsed on Bills of Lading), which the said

Merchant s bind *themselves* to ship on board said Vessel, not exceeding what she can

reasonably stow and carry over and above her Tackle, Apparel, Provisions, and Furniture; and being

so loaded, shall therewith proceed to *Charlestown*

and deliver the same according to Bills of Lading, on being Freight, at the rate of *4/2*

Say Four shillings + twopence per Ton of 20 Cwts. delivered

with 1º (One Penny) gratuity to the master

In full of all port charges, pilotage, and all charges usually borne by the Ship.

(Restraint of Princes and Rulers, the Act of God, the Queen's Enemies, Fire, and all and every
other Dangers and Accidents of the Seas, Rivers, and Navigation, of whatever nature or kind soever,
during the said Voyage, always excepted), Accidents, Colliery Strikes, Combinations of Workmen,
and other causes beyond Charterers' control, interfering with loading or discharging, are mutually
excepted in this Charter.

The Freight to be paid on unloading and right delivery of the Cargo in Cash. If required,

£ *10:0:0* to be advanced on signing Bills of Lading, subject to *2½%* for Insurance.

H. Littlejohn

A Commission of *2½%* is due on signing this Charter Party to R. L. ALPINE & Co., by whom
(or their Agents) the Vessel is to be entered and cleared at port of loading, and to report at
Custom House at port of discharge, with Consignees' Brokers on usual terms.

Ship to be loaded *in regular Colliery turn (Steamers excepted)*

and *30* Tons per working day for discharging the said Ship, according to the custom of the port
of discharge, Sundays and legal or local holidays excepted in both cases, and *any* days on

demurrage, over and above the said lying days, to be at the rate of £ *2.0.0* per day.

Penalty for non-performance of this agreement, estimated amount of Freight.

Witness, *James Armour*   *William Jones*

Witness,   *R. L. Alpine Co*
                               30/7/91

We Certify that the Original Charter-party is in our possession.

A typical charter party document for the three-masted wooden schooner Annie Crossfield *which was owned by J Fisher & Sons of Barrow. She had been built in 1883 at Carrickfergus by P Rodgers with a tonnage of 90 net and dimensions of 94.3ft x 22.5ft x 9.5ft.*
(Private collection)

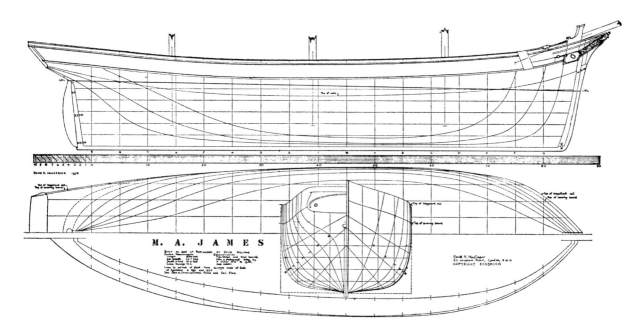

Lines plan of the M A James *drawn by the author from lines he took off the hull, to outside of the plank, at Appledore in 1951 and 1954. Schooner built at Portmadoc in 1900. The figurehead, trailboards and rudder were reconstructed.*

General arrangement, deck beams and bulwark elevation of M A James *drawn by the author from surveys he made of the hull at Appledore in 1951 and 1954. All deck fittings except the windlass were reconstructed, based on photographs taken aboard pre-1939, and also with the assistance of Captain W J Slade.*

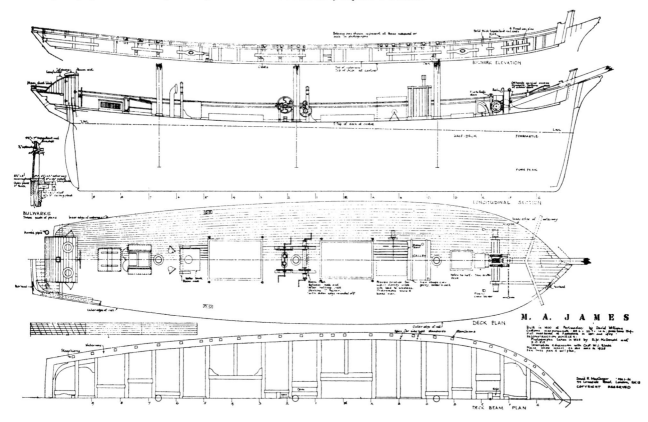

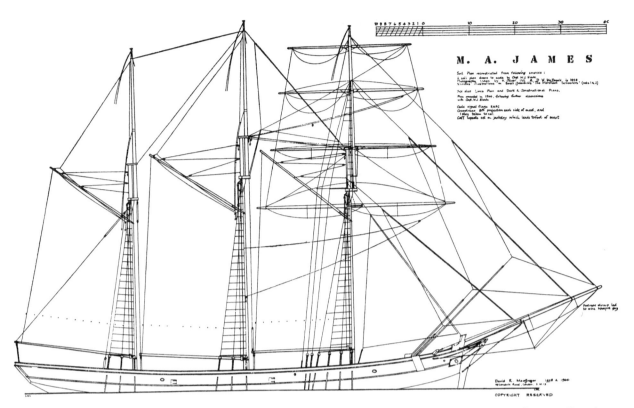

Above: Sail and rigging plan of M A James *drawn by the author, using the sheer elevation of the hull in the lines plan. All spars, sails and rigging reconstructed, principally based on a sail plan drawn to scale by Captain W J Slade, and also from photographs taken pre-1939.*

Below: Interior of M A James *on 7 June 1954, after removal of ceiling planking and rider keelson, looking aft towards sternpost. In spite of her derelict condition, this photograph suggests what the hold of this lovely schooner could have looked like when she was under construction.* (Author)

The crew takes a well-earned rest aboard the M A James *at Padstow in the 1930s whilst unloading coal. The master, George Slade, is second from the left. The plans of this three-masted schooner are reproduced on page 109.* (MacGregor Collection)

was after her arrival on this passage or else after another one in the same year that Heywood's Branch of the Bank of Liverpool wrote to Credit Lyonnais in London on 1 February 1896 requesting them 'to give bail for the sum of £1500 to the Government Authority of Bilbao guaranteeing payment of duties in respect of a cargo of Codfish by the vessel *Little Secret* consigned to Alloqui for account of C T Bowring & Co of Liverpool'. Long-hand copies were made of all letters sent from offices and the post was so rapid that business could be quickly expedited.

The three-masted schooners sailing out of Portmadoc in the thirty or so years before the First World War, which were built especially for the arduous Newfoundland trade, earned the sobriquet of 'Western Ocean Yachts'. They were lofty vessels carrying double topsails and a topgallant on a tall fore topmast, four headsails on a high-steeved bowsprit, with high narrow gaff sails. Using the lines of the *M A James* as a guide, it can readily be seen that the hull possessed a big sheer with a short convex entrance and a longer, somewhat hollow, run with powerful quarters; the midship breadth was kept well forward, and the whole body of the schooner narrowed-in from the mainmast to the stern, thus minimizing the breadth of the square stern at the end of the long counter. The *M A James* cost £2000 to construct and equip or £6.12 per ton on 124.07 gross tons. Basil Greenhill has estimated that there were about fifty schooners of this type built either at Portmadoc or elsewhere. He and I took lines off the *M A James* in 1949 and I drew them out, but was not satisfied with the result. Accordingly, I visited the schooner again in 1951 and 1954 and took off the lines more carefully. I also took the opportunity to measure the deck beams, bulwarks and all surviving fittings. From this I drew out the lines again, and another plan was produced of the deck layout and deck beams. Then, a sail plan was reconstructed, based on a plan drawn by Captain W J Slade, augmented by the use of photographs and his knowledge of the vessel.

The First World War changed everything. Steam coasters, the internal combus-

Aboard the three-masted schooner Mary Barrow *on a passage from Glasgow to Truro in 1937, under the command of Captain P Mortenzen. She has a square sail set from the lower yard and a raffee topsail above. By this date, the use of square canvas was rapidly disappearing from coastal sailing vessels around the British Isles.* (Courtesy of Mark Myers from the Michael Bouquet Collection)

tion engine and the spreading railways concentrated cargo-handling to the larger ports and closed down the smaller ones, including the quays to be found in rivers and estuaries. Horse-drawn carts no longer queued up beside Blakeney Quay nor were they driven at low water on to the wet sand of St Ives' harbour when coal was being discharged from ketches and schooners. Economy was the watchword and auxiliary diesel engines were being installed everywhere, lofty spars were being shortened and crews reduced in number.

Before closing this chapter, mention should be made of the few four-masted schooners built in Great Britain. Two were built of steel in Scotland for Hawaiian registry, the *Americana* in 1892 and the *Honolulu* in 1896. The latter was a bald-headed fore-and-after of 1080 tons. The *Americana* of 901 tons was built for the lumber trade, and according to a photograph in the *American Neptune* (Vol II) was first rigged with topmasts on each mast, a single lower yard on the foremast, and a lower yard and double topsail yards on the mainmast. Built the same year was the *Rimac* of 858 tons, and she was probably first rigged as a topgallant yard schooner, but four years later she was altered to a rig similar to *Americana*. Reid of Port Glasgow, who was her builder, had constructed the steel-hulled *Tacora* in 1888 as a four-masted topgallant yard schooner of 828 tons, but re-rigged her later as a barquentine.

Three-masted schooners constructed with a steel hull had been built, of which the *Result* (1892) is a survivor, and she is now preserved near Belfast, having been hauled out of the water at the Folk Museum. She was designed to sail fast and without ballast if necessary, and not to draw too much; her proportion of beams to length was 4.7 to 1; she displaced 88 tons net and 122 tons gross in 1895, two years after she was built at Carrickfergus, on the north shore of Belfast Lough. She was owned by the Ashburner family until 1909 when their fleet was sold and dispersed. During the First World War she was a 'Q ship' and was twice in action against German submarines. In 1946 she was equipped with a more powerful 120-horsepower engine but still used her sails, and I remember seeing her under sail off Bideford Bar in August 1948, waiting for the tide to serve, before she could go up to the quay at Fremington to discharge her cargo of coal. In the Richmond Yard at Appledore, James and Frank Cock constructed four three-masted schooners built of steel in the years 1904-09, and all were of about 99 tons.

Yachts | *12*

IT SEEMS not inconsistent with history to believe that the yacht was first adopted in Holland in the opening years of the seventeenth century where it was admired and the pleasures it gave were greatly appreciated. When the Dutch word *jaght* was used in connection with hunting it could indicate swiftness, and correspondingly *jaght schip* could imply a swift ship, and from such a source the English word 'yacht' is derived. Such a craft had one mast with a gaff or sprit supporting the mainsail and was rigged as a sloop with a yard and bowsprit; if for royal pleasures, the hull would have carving and lavish decoration applied. As a King, Charles II was an enthusiastic patron of yachting and many of the larger yachts in his reign were rigged as square-rigged ketches. Examples of a few schooner-rigged yachts are given in Chapter 2, together with illustrations, but to what extent the two-masted schooner-rig was employed in English yachts is unknown. It probably followed closely the adoption of the schooner rig in commercial vessels which would imply that, apart from occasional examples, it did not become popular until after 1815. Pleasure craft rigged with two gaff sails were undoubtedly sailed in estuaries and coastal waters, but for country gentlemen they were generally day boats without cabins. The first yacht club in England was the Cumberland Fleet, founded in 1775, and named after the Duke of Cumberland; members were able to fly the White Ensign but with the red cross of St George omitted.

This lithograph by Thomas G Dutton, dated 1831, shows the two-topsail schooner yacht Dolphin hove-to. The fitting of a square topsail and topgallant on each mast was also a form of rig then employed on opium clippers in the China Sea, and had at one time been popular with privateers. This yacht, of 217 tons, was owned by George Ackers from 1831 to 1839. (Private collection)

Above: The fore-and-aft schooner Janette *off the Eddystone lighthouse. Her fore yard from which she could set a square sail is lowered close to the deck. Perhaps she was owned by the 5th Earl of Egremont in the 1840s. (Courtesy of the Parker Gallery)*

Right: The three-masted schooner Brilliant *was owned by George H Ackers from 1839 to 1862 and this wash drawing depicts her under sail with guns run out, naval fashion. Various tonnages are assigned to her, but her register was 292 tons; 393 tons was possibly old measurement; 480 tons in Hunt's Yacht list was presumably Thames Measurement. Her builder was Rubie. The fitting of square sails on the main topmast is none too common; if the foremast had been square-rigged she would have been a jackass barque. The royal yards have not been drawn here. (MacGregor Collection)*

Two clubs were founded in 1815: one was the Yacht Club after a meeting in London and two years later it was allowed to prefix its name with 'Royal'; the other was the Dee Yacht Club, becoming 'Royal' in 1847. The Royal Yacht Club established itself at Cowes in 1825 by leasing a club house. Four years later it was allowed to wear the correct White Ensign and in 1833 William IV renamed it 'The Royal Yacht Squadron'. Meanwhile other clubs were being founded and members of the Cumberland Fleet reconstituted themselves as the Thames Yacht Club in 1823, becoming 'Royal' in 1830. The old Cumberland Fleet was disbanded in 1831.

Early examples of schooners of this period which were owned by members of the Squadron included the *Jack o'Lantern* of 140 tons, owned by Thomas Assheton-Smith in 1824, the *Galatea* of 179 tons owned by Mr Talbot in 1827, the *Fly* of 73 tons owned by the Marquis of Buckingham in 1815, the *Emma* of 132 tons owned by Sir William Curtis in 1824, and there were a number of others. All schooners at this date, and the majority of them up to 1850, carried square sails on the fore topmast and a few even carried them on the mainmast as well; in addition, a square sail

Lines, general arrangement and sail plan of the yacht America *as first rigged. She was designed by George Steers and built in New York in 1851 with a length on deck of 95ft 6in and registered 170 tons (New York Custom House). Reproduced from plate 81 in* Admiral Pâris, *Souvenirs de Marine Conservés.*

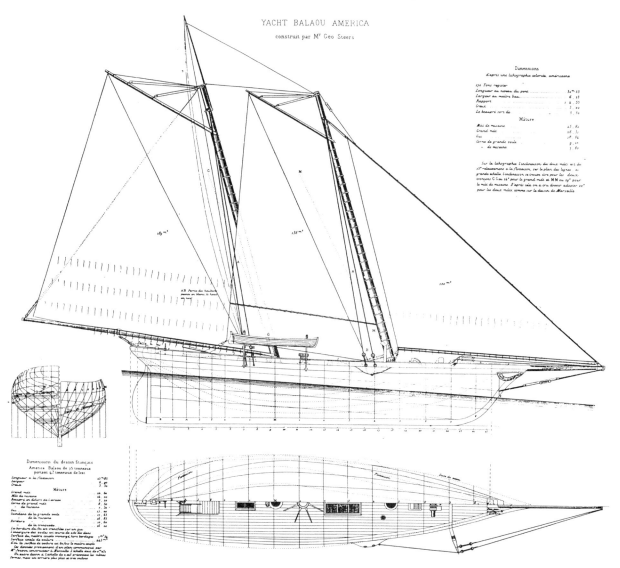

YACHT BALAOU AMERICA
construit par Mr Geo Steers

The American schooner yacht Sappho, *having rounded the marker vessel off St Catherine's, is running off before the wind, and the British* Cambria *is approaching the marker boat. The American vessel was of 394 tons and usually set jib-headed topsails; she also had a bowsprit, jibboom and dolphin striker; the British yacht of 193 tons usually set topsails with a head yard and carried a spike bowsprit. Tonnages by Royal Thames Yacht Club rules. Engraving from* Illustrated London News *(1870).*

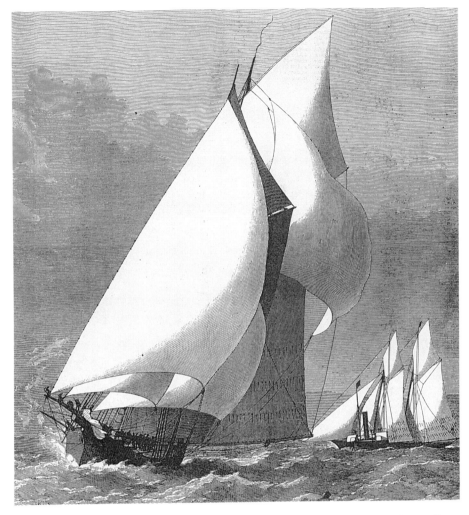

was set from the fore yard and also studdingsails outside the topsail and topgallant, so that they presented a similar appearance to some of the American privateers that were once encountered on the high seas. Some unusual craft included the *Xarifa* owned by Lord Wilton which was supposedly an ex-slaver; an unnamed three-masted Bermudian-rigged schooner with a single headsail and a long lean hull about 50ft long, painted by J Lynn in 1843 (Heckstall-Smith, *Yachts & Yachting in Contemporary Art*, plate XL); the three-masted schooner *Brilliant* of 292 tons which crossed topsail and topgallant yards on both fore and main topmasts (page 114); and at least two three-masted luggers one of which was the *New Moon* with a vertical stem and no sheer (engraving in the *Illustrated London News c*1859).

The *Brilliant* was owned by George H Ackers who was a member of the Royal Yacht Squadron from 1837 to 1871. He began with the schooner *Dolphin* which had topsails and topgallants on both masts; then he had the *Brilliant* from 1839 to 1862, and in one illustration she has three yards on the mizen topmast as well as on main and fore. A few fore-and-aft schooners were making their appearance in the 1840s and their popularity increased with the launch of the *America* in 1851.

John Stevens, Commodore of the New York Yacht Club, his brother and four of their friends purchased a schooner yacht that was under construction early in 1851 in

Left: Unidentified schooner yacht heeling over as she slices through the water. (Private collection)

Below: Sail plan and midship section of the auxiliary three-masted schooner Diana *which was built for James Lamont of Glasgow, so that he could indulge his hunting exploits in Arctic waters. Built in 1869 by Alexander Stephen & Sons at Glasgow of composite construction with a tonnage of 189 gross and dimensions of 115ft 0in x 21ft 6in x 12ft 7in. This was the sort of rig fitted to the* Brilliant *(page 114).* (MacGregor Collection)

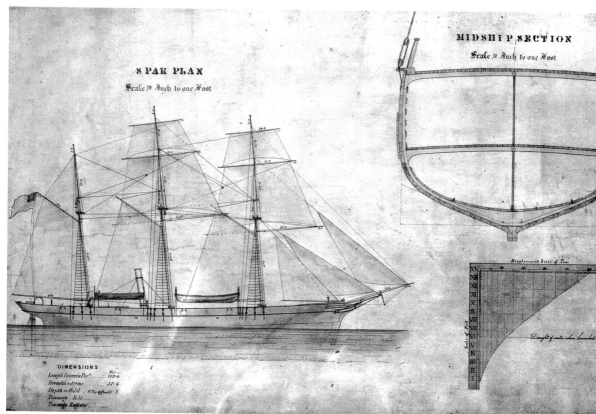

In this dramatic picture of wind-filled canvas, the American yacht Dauntless *has a quartering wind, filling the big square sail which blankets the headsails. She was built at Mystic, Connecticut, in 1869 and she was of 299 tons Thames Measurement.* (Private collection)

The schooner Westward *between the 'J' class gaff cutters,* Lulworth *(left) and* Britannia. *The* Westward, *ex-*Hamburg II, *ex-*Westward, *was designed and built by Herreshoff at Bristol, Rhode Island, in 1910, and was raced in Britain by T B F Davis. She registered 180 tons gross or 323 tons Thames Measurement and was 135ft long overall.* (MacGregor Collection)

the yard of William H Brown of New York and which had been designed by George Steers who was then working for Brown. This was the famous yacht *America* and as was the custom in many shipyards, Steers designed the hull by building a half-model. Her length on deck was 95ft 6in, extreme beam was 23ft 0in and she was of $210^{10}/_{94}$ tons by British old measurement. Her hull-form showed steep deadrise, a long concave entrance with maximum beam well aft, and a shortish and fuller run with hollows in the lower body. She drew 4ft more aft than forward. She was rigged as a fore-and-aft schooner with two masts of approximately equal height, a topmast on the mainmast only, and a short bowsprit. The two gaff sails were held to the masts with numerous hoops; the foresail was boomless, the mainsail and the huge jib or fore staysail were both laced to long booms; the sails were of cotton and could set very flat, whereas the English sails were of flax, cut full and were loose-footed.

Launched in May 1851, the *America* sailed across the Atlantic and reached Cowes

in August, and on the 22nd of that month was entered for a race round the Isle of Wight for a cup valued at £100. The course was in a clockwise direction and thirteen other yachts challenged in the light wind, but unfortunately the *Volante* and the fast *Arrow* collided whilst tacking inshore and the latter ran aground. The equally fast *Alarm* stayed by to give assistance, with the result that the three fastest British defenders were out of the race. Eventually the *America* ghosted along before the light westerly breeze and crossed the finishing line off Cowes, eight minutes ahead of the small cutter *Aurora*, which was almost unnoticed. The cup was taken back to New York and up until the Second World War, sixteen challengers had crossed the Atlantic in vain attempts to wrest the trophy from the New York Yacht Club and take it back to England.

When the *America* was under the ownership of Lord de Blaquiere in 1852, an English yachtsman commented on the 'almost mop-handle diminutiveness of her tiller' and added that he had 'steered her when going seven knots close hauled and in some Bay of Naples swell, standing to leeward of the tiller and pressing against it with my little finger only' (quoted by B Heckstall-Smith in *Yachts & Yachting in Contemporary Art* 1925). Of the English yachts that were remodelled as a result of the *America*'s win, perhaps none made a greater attempt to copy her than the cutter *Alarm* which had her forward end lengthened by 20ft to give her a hollow entrance, thus increasing the tonnage from 193 to 248 tons; simultaneously she was re-rigged as a schooner to imitate the *America* in appearance and detail. Another imitation was the Swedish schooner yacht *Sverige* which was to be seen in British waters in 1852.

For cruising purposes, schooners were still preferred to have square topsails but for racing the pure fore-and-aft rig was rapidly becoming essential for the twenty years or so up to the mid-1870s. The writer of an article in *Hunt's Yachting Magazine* (1854 Vol III) considered that in spite of the popularity of topsail schooners, they

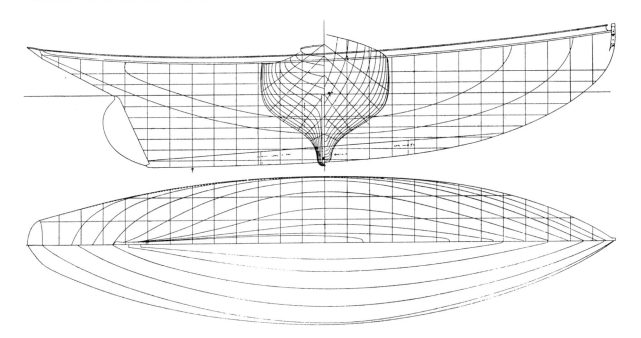

Lines plan of auxiliary schooner yacht Morwenna *built at Shoreham in 1914 of 28 tons Thames Measurement. Designed by Linton Hope. Plan reproduced in* Yachting Monthly *(Vol XVII September 1914).*

were inefficient in turning to windward owing to the 'great amount of rigging' although it 'was a very useful sail in backing the vessel round, when staying in a head sea'. He was in favour of the triatic stay between the two mast heads instead of a stay on either side leading forward from the mainmast hounds which had constantly to be set up or slacked off; another item he favoured was the huge staysail like a 'cutter's fore-sail', working in a gooseneck at the outer end of the bowsprit.

The heyday of the racing schooners produced a constant stream of new vessels as one sleek craft after another slid down the launching ways, and there was an increasing amount of international competitiveness. In December 1866, three American schooners, the *Henrietta*, *Vesta* and *Fleetwing*, raced across the Atlantic from Sandy Hook to Cowes for a stake of £10,000, which *Henrietta* won with a time of 13 days 21 hours. In 1868 and again in 1870, the American *Sappho* and the British *Cambria* raced both around the Isle of Wight and in the Channel. The American schooner was 394 tons Thames Measurement and the *Cambria* somewhat smaller at 193. The *Illustrated London News* had some splendid engravings signed by E[dward] W[eedon]of the races with the vessels often at close quarters in whole-sail breezes. There were a small number of big three-masted cruising yachts such as *Sunbeam*, *Czarina* and *Aello II* but they usually had auxiliary engines. The *Sunbeam* made a celebrated voyage around the world in 1876-77 and her longest day's run under sail alone was 270 miles, made in the South Atlantic. Another favourite cruising ground was in Arctic waters, although this tended to be more like a shooting expedition. *Hunt's Universal Yacht List* is a useful compendium as it gives sailmakers' names, house flags, dates when yachts were altered and clubs to which owners belonged, as well as the usual measurements.

Although costs had not increased much during the nineteenth century, they were absurdly cheap compared with today. One owner, writing in the 1890s, commented that to fit out a schooner for a summer cruise to the Mediterranean lasting three months, to provide all necessary stores, gear and equipment, to pay the skipper and

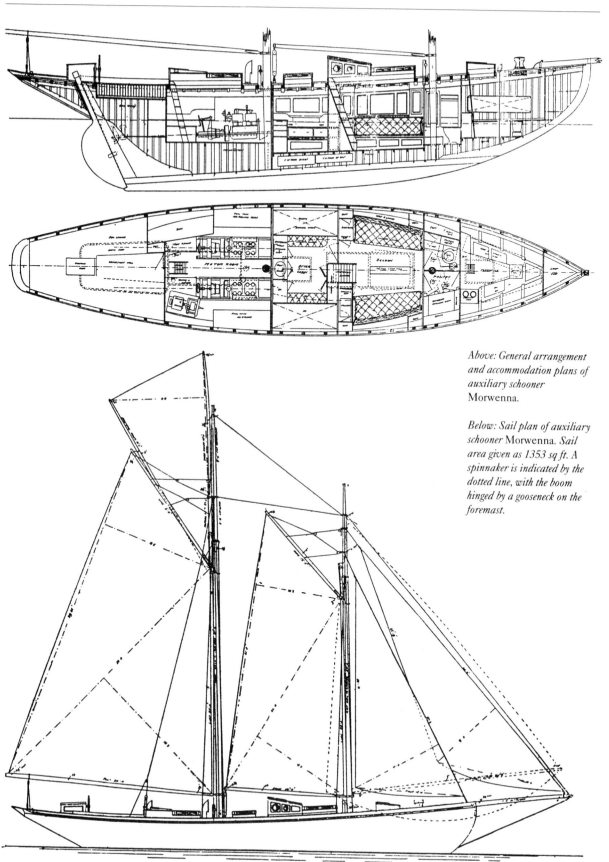

Above: General arrangement and accommodation plans of auxiliary schooner Morwenna.

Below: Sail plan of auxiliary schooner Morwenna. *Sail area given as 1353 sq ft. A spinnaker is indicated by the dotted line, with the boom hinged by a gooseneck on the foremast.*

crew, to assist friends travelling overland to and from the vessel, plus all the other expenses, made a big hole in £1000. Many of the schooners had long lives and one of the largest schooners afloat in 1905 without an auxiliary engine was probably the *Livonia* of 128 tons which had been built in 1871 as a challenger for the 'America's Cup'.

The shape of schooners had changed by the beginning of the twentieth century and the cruising yachts were requiring auxiliary engines. An example of one launched on the eve of the First World War was the *Morwenna*. She was designed by Linton Hope and built by Stow & Son of Shoreham in 1914 for Mr J Malcolm of Fowey. Her dimensions were 55ft length overall, 12ft beam, 6.7ft draught, and she

Looking aft aboard the Morwenna *with Mr Barling, the owner, standing on the companionway stairs.* (Courtesy of I M Barling)

displaced 28 tons Thames Measurement and 20 tons gross. She was powered by two 30hp Thornycroft paraffin engines to give a speed of 8.5 knots. As the plan on page 121 shows, she had a sizeable sail area of 1353 sq ft and was an attractive craft with a curved stem, a long counter, pole masts and a short bowsprit. There was over 8 tons of lead in the keel, and she was constructed to Lloyd's rules with oak frames, elm planking on bottom and teak on the topsides; teak was also used for the skylights and companionways, and the deck planking was Kauri pine. She had done some ocean cruising between the two Wars and the figures '124' on the peak of her mainsail indicated that she had also raced at some stage. The owner–not the original one–having been killed in an air raid in London, she was bought by Mr I T Barling and laid up near Salcombe during the War. She was fitted out after the end of hostilities for less than £1000; fortunately the sails, made of flax, had been carefully stored and were found to be in first class condition. The family cruised to France and Ireland in her until she was sold in 1957.

Since 1918, schooner yachts have been built in limited numbers although usually in smaller sizes than formerly, and many have been constructed in the United States, where the gaff sail has retained its popularity. Ports such as Camden, Maine, have quite a fleet of 'dude' schooners for holiday cruises which help to keep the gaff-rigged tradition alive.

ALTHOUGH THE schooner rig appears to have started in Holland in the early part of the seventeenth century, it would seem to have gone out of favour in the eighteenth century because, out of the eighty-four engravings of various rigs published by G Groenewegen at Rotterdam in 1789, only one depicts a schooner, a *Kanonneer boot*, with square topsails on each mast. Prior to 1815, all illustrations of Dutch schooners show them to have been armed.

In the first half of the nineteenth century, North European round-sterned galliots and square-sterned galleases set three square sails on the mainmast – deep square-sail from the lower yard, topsail, topgallant – and also a gaff sail. On the mizen, where the topmast was sometimes as high above the deck as was the main topmast, there was a narrower gaff sail and a topsail. Schooners had a very similar rig, of course, but with a bigger mainsail. The plan of a schooner-rigged *kof* of 1841 gives an indication of the rig (page 126). From the plans in Hans Szymanski's book *Deutsche Segelschiffe*, it can be seen that the galleas and galliot were both full-bodied

A Dutch gunboat sailing close-hauled with a square topsail on each mast. This engraving by G Groenewegen was published at Rotterdam in 1789.

craft but that the schooner had a sharper entrance and run, and he reproduces a painting of the schooner *Ferdinand* of Stettin (*c*1820) with topsails and topgallants on each mast. In this case, the parrals of the topsail yards slide on the doubling of the topmast below the lower mast cap, which was how the *Glasgow* was rigged, as described in Chapter 6. The *schunerbrigg* was popular in northern Europe and the *George Canning* of Stettin, pictured as figure 141 in Szymanski's book as entering Palermo in 1834, has a fore royal mast fidded abaft the topgallant mast, but carries a foresail set on gaff and boom with a luff almost as long as on the mainsail. The large square sail set from the fore yard was regularly carried and the *Maria* of Flensburg had one set in 1860 together with a studdingsail.

In Denmark it was the sloop and brig which were the popular rigs for trade in north European waters in the early part of the nineteenth century, but gradually the schooner began to appear so that by the 1850s they were being launched in considerable numbers, and some sloops were being lengthened and having a second mast added. Although many of the schooners were '*jagt*-built' with bluff bows and vertical stems, a change was coming, and the first clipper in the Svendborg area was the *Thuroe* of 1856. Such vessels carried a topsail and topgallant with a square sail from the foreyard, as well as a full suit of studdingsails. Many such vessels traded to and from the West Indies; others went to Eastern waters and spent their entire life there, never returning home after once beginning their maiden passage.

During the 1860s, the first three-masted schooners began to appear and several were built to carry square sails on the main topmast as well as on the fore. Two of this rig were the *Familia* of Troense, Denmark, built in 1851, and the *Mathilde* of

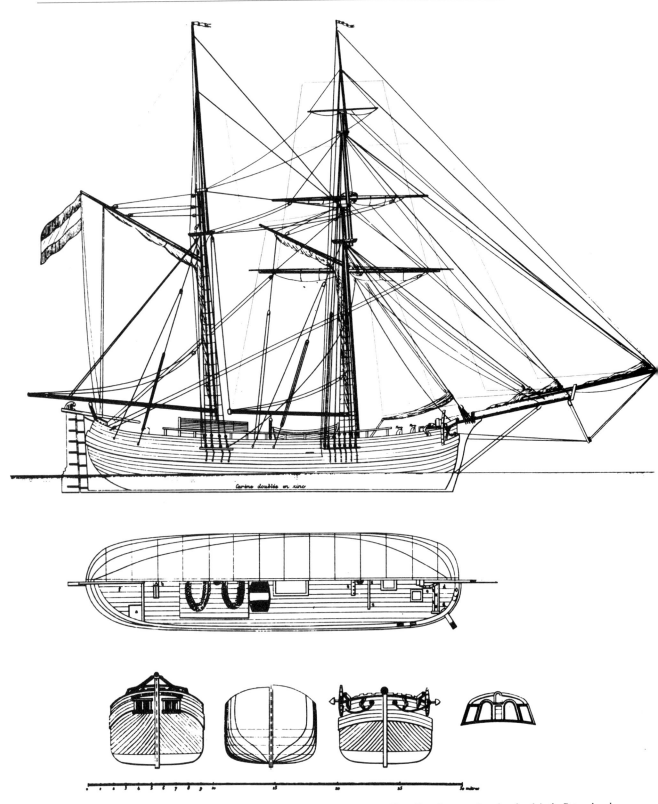

Lines, deck plan, sail and rigging plan of a Dutch kof *dated 1841 and of 250 tons. The sail outlines are dotted rather faintly. Reproduced from Admiral Pâris,* Souvenirs de Marine, *plate 45. With her three-piece foremast, she could be classified as a schooner-brigantine, although she has no square foresail outlined.*

Above: This portrait of the Urania *was painted on glass by an Antwerp artist. She was built at Kiel in 1854 and has a modified form of an 'Aberdeen bow'. The weather clew of the large square foresail is boomed out by a spar from the foremast.* (Photograph of painting in MacGregor Collection)

Left: The Danish Maren *was really a fore-and-aft schooner but did carry a fore yard, which is here lowered. She had an old hull which was constructed in 1815 at Arnis on the River Schlei, now part of Germany, but she was then rigged as a* jagt *or sloop. In 1884 she was sold to owners in the Danish island of Aero and six years later was re-rigged as a schooner.* (F Holm-Petersen Collection)

Above: The three-masted schooner Zenitha *is seen under construction in the yard of J Ring Andersen at Svendborg, Denmark, where she is going to be launched in 1904, bow first. The planking has reached the level of the covering board and the bulwark stanchions stick upwards like a fence. Her measurements were 114.5ft x 26.9ft x 11.8ft and 195 tons net.* (F Holm-Petersen Collection)

Below: An unidentified French topsail schooner at Paimpol, Brittany, with every sail set except the fore staysail, which has been furled and then hoisted up its stay. The deep fore topsail is a roller-reefing variety, with the sail rolling around a subsidiary yard as the topsail yard is lowered. Copied from a picture postcard. (MacGregor Collection)

Above: The master, mate and crew aboard the three-masted topsail schooner Yrsa. *She was built at Marstal in 1902 of 100 tons net with a length of 90.7ft. The chain cable is brought along the deck beside the hatch, from the windlass, and goes down the spurling pipe into the chain locker at the left of this picture. (F Holm-Petersen Collection)*

Top right: Captain S Jürgensen taking a sight aboard the three-masted schooner Frem, *which was built at Marstal, Denmark, for the Newfoundland trade in which at one time 125 Danish schooners were engaged. Her year of construction was 1919 and she was of 119 tons net. This photograph was taken at the stern, looking forward to where her square sail is set; she carried no topsail yards. (F Holm-Petersen Collection)*

Left:The double-ended three-masted schooner in the centre has the name Anna Madre *of 'Genova' (Genoa) on her name board and as this is from a picture postcard, the date can be narrowed down to post-1905. However, no such vessel is listed in the* Bureau Veritas *'Register' for 1906 or 1910, although the 'Répertoire Général' for 1921 lists a two-masted vessel of this name, built in 1906 of 62 tons and registered at Livorno (Leghorn). Presumably she was built for a special trade. (MacGregor Collection)*

A sail plan of the Phoenix *dated 1873 from the yard of J Ring Andersen in Svendborg. The date of build is given as 1874 and tonnage was stated as 115. The staysails are draw as by a sailmaker, indicating the cut of the sails; the horizontal line on the upper topsail indicates a row of reef points.* (F Holm-Petersen Collection)

Kiel, built in 1863. From Norway there was a large trade in carrying ice to the southern ports of England and likewise to France and Spain; Norwegian schooners also traded to most ports of the world.

By the 1890s, many of the fine three-masted topgallant-yard schooners that were being launched from Scandinavian and north European shipyards were similar to the Western Ocean Yachts. The Danish schooners of this type crossed four yards on the foremast and were lofty vessels with pronounced sheer, having square sterns and clipper bows. They were often broad in the beam with appreciable deadrise and had a sharp convex entrance and run. Counter sterns were usually square, but J Ring Anderson's yard at Svendborg was famous for its graceful round counter sterns. A vessel built at Marstal could be recognised anywhere by its plain curved stem, square tuck stern – the lower part of which was varnished – and outside rudder. These schooners often had a standing gaff on the foremast, and the sail was then hooped to both gaff and mast. Frode Holm-Petersen has chronicled the sailing vessels of Denmark in his many books which are well-illustrated and a good source of information.

Apart from their voyages across the North Sea and the North Atlantic, these three-masted schooners were to be found in ports throughout the world. In 1905, for example, the Svendborg schooner *Dagny* called at the Falkland Islands, and two years later the *Dannebrog* was lost off the Brazilian coast. These schooners continued to be built in large numbers until 1914 and some were even built between the Wars.

Denmark was unique as being the only country outside of the United States where large numbers of four-masted schooners were constructed, starting in 1913 and finishing in 1924. In these years, according to a list compiled by Jens Malling and published in *Log Chips*, no less than fifty-one four-masters were launched, mostly in 1919 and 1920. Seventeen were built of steel and the remainder of wood, thirty-four had auxiliary engines and the majority were in the 300 to 400 tons range, which was small by American standards. About half-a-dozen carried four yards on the foremast but most had only a single yard on this mast, although fidded topmasts were normal.

In Chapter 14 are to be found references to the big American schooners bought by Norwegian owners during the First World War and also to the five-masters ordered by the French Government from the Pacific Coast shipyards.

In France, one class of two-masted schooner which resembled the fisherman or *morutier* was the *caboteur* which did not have the deep heel, yet was a fast vessel, being sailed by a crew of five. In rig arrangement she closely resembled the *morutier* with a deep roller-reefing topsail which first made its appearance about 1910. Prior to this, double topsails were set. Although few, if any, schooners were built after 1914, they can still be remembered under sail in the Bristol Channel in the 1930s

An unidentified vessel alongside the quay in Tyne Dock at South Shields. She looks like a three-masted schooner or barquentine, and the corner of the deckhouse on the right would certainly not be found on a British vessel. The monkey fo'c'sle is clearly shown, with the inboard ends of the catheads meeting at the pawl post. There is a spike bowsprit with a dolphin striker some distance out, by the jib stay, and not where the bobstay is secured. (Petersen Collection, South Shields Public Libraries & Museums)

An impressive sight of the harbour at Marstal, Denmark, taken c1921-22, with the schooners tightly packed in serried ranks. In the front row, there is a four-master with her lower yard cock-billed. Most of the schooners cross a topgallant yard above double topsail yards. The exterior of the hulls were commonly black, and the deck fittings and bulwarks in-board were mostly white.
(Copied from picture postcard)

Below: A motorised ketch under construction in J Ring Andersen's yard at Svendborg, Denmark, in September 1953. All the frames are in place except for the forward cant frames. The steam chest for bending the planking is on the extreme left, and the scrieve board, on which the body plan is drawn and where the frames are assembled, is on the extreme right. (Author)

An unidentified three-masted schooner photographed by the late Peter M Wood when he was making a passage on the barque Alastor *during the 1930s. The spike bowsprit is remarkably long and without any dolphin striker. All sail is set in the light breeze with the exception of the fore staysail which is furled; even the main topmast staysail and the weather-side of the square sail are set.* (MacGregor Collection)

The three-masted topsail schooner Penola, *ex-Naraho, in dry dock on the River Tyne. This vessel was built at Kerity, France, in 1908 and became registered in London c1934 when her original name must have been changed. Perhaps it was then she was fitted out in London to take members of the Graham Land Expedition to the southern hemisphere. By 1937 she was owned in South Australia and was equipped with 100bhp engines and measured 108.0ft x 24.1ft x 11.6ft, 138 net and 166 gross tons. By 1939 she was owned in Northumberland and her net tonnage had shrunk to 84 tons. Her bow appears to have been strengthened against ice.* (Petersen Collection, South Shields Public Libraries & Museums)

Above: The staysail schooner
Stormie Seas, *49ft long, was
used by Peter Throckmorton
for exploration in the
Mediterranean.* (Peter
Throckmorton)

*Above: There were altogether five schooners of identical rig and size built in 1921-22 by Krupp of Kiel for
the Bremen firm of Vinnen, and although all five names ended in 'Vinnen' each began with a different
Christian name. The one pictured here is the* Carl Vinnen, *built in 1922 with a tonnage of 1524 net and a
hull length of 261.8ft. Her diesel engines were fitted aft. This photograph probably shows her full suit of
sails, although whether she set any topmast staysails is uncertain.* (MacGregor Collection)

Left: A Scandinavian schooner drying her sails whilst at anchor off West Appledore, North Devon, with her bows still pointing towards Bideford Bar. She has not yet unloaded her cargo of timber which still encumbers her decks. (MacGregor Collection, from a picture postcard)

when they were taking cargoes of potatoes, onions and pit props to South Wales, and returning to Brittany with coal. One which survived the War was the *Roscovite* which lay for many years in Svendborg harbour under the name of *Arken*.

It is difficult to track down all the other four or five-masted schooners built in other European harbours, but the four-master *Abraham* of 315 tons was built in 1893 at Windau, Russia; two five-masters of about 1200 tons each were built in Portugal in 1919, both of wood; two auxiliary four-masters were built in Holland in 1920; and in Italy in 1922 the five-master *Perseveranza* was built of concrete.

At Kiel in 1921-22, Krupp constructed five five-masted schooners with auxiliary

Below: The Danish four-master Ingeborg, ex-*Niels Hansen, went ashore at Weyborne on the North Norfolk coast, presumably in fog as she does not look damaged and is not lying broadside on to the beach. She was lost in 1926 but it is not clear if this was the actual occasion. She was built in 1916 and changed her name within twelve months. She was constructed at Svendborg, Denmark, by J Ring Andersen with a length of 139.1ft and of 373 tons gross; she had a diesel engine. She seems a pure fore-and-aft schooner without so much as a single yard on her foremast.* (MacGregor Collection)

The waterfront of Salonica in 1954, according to a postcard sent me by Basil Greenhill, the message of which appears in the text.

engines and built of steel. All of them crossed four yards on the foremast and the mizen mast, but none on the main, jigger or spanker masts. This rig arrangement made them famous as did their names which all ended in 'Vinnen', derived from their owner's name, F A Vinnen Ltd of Bremen: they were the *Adolphe Vinnen*, *Carl Vinnen*, *Christle Vinnen*, *Susanne Vinnen* and *Werner Vinnen*. They were intended to be identical sister ships and in the case of the *Werner Vinnen* the measurements were 261.5ft x 44.4ft x 19.2ft, 1859 tons gross and 1548 tons net, quarter deck 83ft long, foc's'le 55ft long. The *Adolphe Vinnen* was driven ashore on the Cornish coast in 1923 on her maiden passage from the Elbe to load Welsh coal at Barry. She was in ballast and although her master, Captain Willy Muller, was an experienced master of deep-water square-riggers, it may be he was as yet unfamiliar with this new schooner. It has been said that an auxiliary engine gives a feeling of security but lacks the necessary power in an emergency. However, the other sister ships fared better and earned good profits for their owners.

In Italy and other Mediterranean countries, the schooner was used extensively in the last century and in this, but picture postcards show that the brigantine predominated prior to 1914, particularly in Italy. At Palma de Majorca, two and three-masted schooners survived into recent years and at least one was constructed as late as 1950. They were still much in use in Greece in 1954 because Basil Greenhill sent me a postcard that year from Salonica on which he wrote:

This place is crawling with schooners. There are almost a dozen schooners and smacks in front of the hotel now, and they come and go every hour. Some of them are very attractive and some give the impression of being very new as well. Topsails are definitely *demodé*. The vogue here is for an enormous area of canvas from gaffs and booms from tall rather lovely pole masts. In Syria they go in for very lofty Bermudas.

The Big Schooners | *14*

AFTER THE American Civil War, the shipyards of Maine produced some splendid medium clippers for deepwater trade, later called 'Down Easters', but the high insurance rates on wooden hulls decreed by Lloyd's favoured iron and steel ships and curtailed the production of square-riggers in Maine after the mid-1880s. Therefore, builders and owners turned to the coastwise trade where there was a growing demand for the transport of coal and wood for house construction in the manufacturing centres of New England. The scene was now set for the creation of the massive multi-masted schooners which were equipped with four, five or six huge gaff sails. As owners called for ever-larger ships to meet the growing demand, shipwrights searched for new ways to bind together the enormous wooden hulls which sometimes exceeded 3000 tons. This shipbuilding programme became so extensive that it was not until 1894 that the tonnage of steamers in the coasting trade exceeded that of sailing vessels.

Launch of the Lucia P Dow *by the Francis Cobb Shipbuilding Co at Rockland, Maine, in 1919 with a gross tonnage of 998. In 1931 she was sold to Canadian owners and stranded the same year; then used as a coal hulk at St John, NB.* (Courtesy of W J Lewis Parker)

Right: Looking forward aboard the four-masted schooner Wm J Lermond. *The helmsman is at the wheel (left) and the top of the big after deckhouse is in front of him. The men look diminutive against the massive masts. She was built at Thomaston, Maine, in 1885 of 888 tons gross.* (Courtesy of W J Lewis Parker)

Below: The four-masted schooner Cutty Sark *was built in 1919 at the end of the shipbuilding boom, and she traded for ten years until abandoned on a passage from Nova Scotia to Bermuda. She measured 609 tons and is here shown with a big deck load of timber that was kept from shifting, partly by stout posts along the bulwarks and partly by chain lashings.* (By courtesy of the Nova Scotia Museum, Halifax)

John Lyman carried out research to determine the earliest four-masted schooners prior to 1880 and submitted three names which turned out to be vessels built for other purposes but subsequently rigged with four masts (*Log Chips* Vol I, July 1949, pp78-79). In 1863 the barge *Victoria* was rebuilt into a four-masted schooner of 344 tons out of San Francisco; the Civil War gunboat *Osceola* was sold in 1867 and renamed *Eliza* of 643 tons, and by 1870 was trading between Boston and Montevideo and was listed as a four-masted schooner and also as a 'quartette'; the third, and best-known example, was the *Weybosset* which was built as a steamer in 1863 and converted to a four-masted schooner in 1879. However, the first schooner actually designed and built with four masts was the *William L White* and Henry Hall described her in his *Report on the Ship-building Industry of the United States*, written in 1882 and published two years later:

In a stiff breeze, the crew are hauling in the jigger sheet on the four-masted schooner Admiral. *She had a beam of 36.2ft and a tonnage of 605, and was built at Coos Bay, Oregon, in 1899. Her deck cargo of timber starts by the jigger mast, on the right. Looking astern, the sea is filled with breaking wave crests. (Courtesy of the National Maritime Museum, San Francisco)*

In 1880 an advance was made in the building of the *William L White*, of Taunton, Massachusetts, at a ship-yard in Bath, Maine. The hull of the vessel was large enough for a Californian. She was 205 feet long on deck, 40 feet beam, and 17 feet deep in the hold, being 309 feet in length over all from the end of the jib-boom to the end of the spanker boom. She registered 996 tons, and was able to carry 1450 tons of anthracite coal. This vessel was rigged as a four-masted schooner. To have fitted her out with three masts would have required such large lower sails that the strain upon the masts would have been destructive, and she was therefore furnished with four, the after spar being called the spanker mast. This divided her 5017 yards of canvas into smaller sails and made her a good schooner, sailing well, easily handled, and requiring a crew of only five men before the mast, besides her

A busy scene in the shipyard of Hall Bros, at Port Blakeley, Washington, presumably situated on narrow Blakeley Harbour which is on the shore of Puget Sound, south of Bainbridge Island. The year is 1902 and people have arrived to witness the launch of the five-masted schooner H K Hall *(left). Two four-masted schooners are on the stocks: in the centre is the* Blakeley *and on the right is the* Caroline. *(Courtesy of the National Maritime Museum, San Francisco)*

two mates and captain. This was the first four-masted schooner built for actual ocean service in America, and probably the first ever so employed in the world, although there is on record a case where a small one was built in England in 1800 for packet service to India . . . [and he goes on to describe the *Transit*, ignoring the fact that she was built with five masts before being reduced to four and anyhow was rigged as a barquentine].

As described above, the *William L White* was built in 1880 by Goss, Sawyer & Packard at Bath, Maine, and after a brief career was lost at sea in November 1882. Henry Hall's description omits to state that the schooner had a centreboard. Her remarkably small crew was only possible because of the steam donkey engine which provided power to handle the heavy gear speedily. It was only in the previous year that Captain David O'Keefe of the schooner *William D Marvel* had suggested that a steam donkey engine be used aboard the larger vessels for working

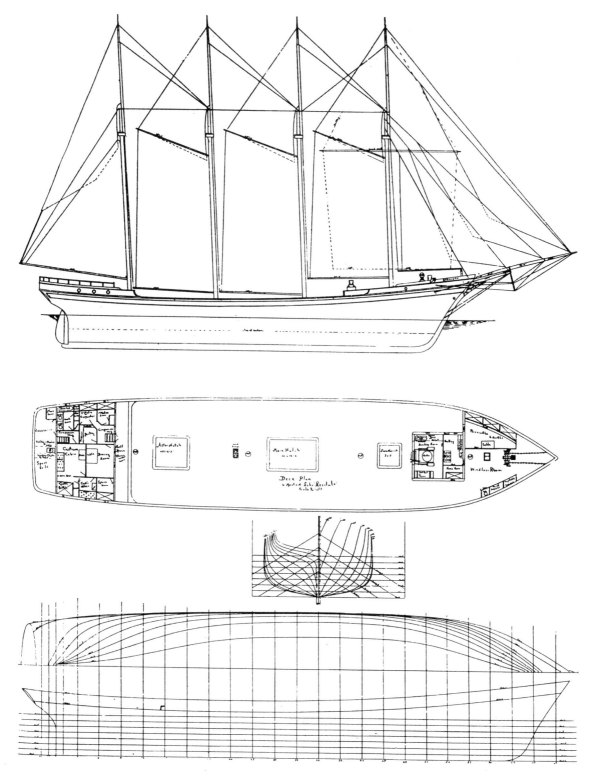

Lines plan, deck layout and sail plan of the Resolute *built in 1902 at Hoquiam, Washington, by Hitchings & Joyce with dimensions of 182.2ft x 39.5ft x 14.2ft and 684 tons gross. Reproduced from plan published in* The Rudder *(Vol XIII June 1902) (see pages 155-6). She was designed to carry 800,000ft of lumber. She had a jib-headed spanker and ringtail topsail which made furling the sail that much easier; there is also a yard on the foremast to set a big square sail. An article accompanying this plan considered that Pacific Coast vessels were 'much better modelled craft than our average eastern vessel'.*

the windlass and pumps, for turning the capstan and hoisting the sails, and the schooner *Josie R Burt* of 760 tons, built at Bath in 1882, was among the first to be equipped with this gear. Using steam power she hoisted all sail, excluding her topmast staysails, and hove in her anchor and 30 fathoms of chain in half-an-hour, while the *Zaccheus Sherman* in company with her but without a steam donkey took half a day to perform the same thing. A head of steam was always ready, even in a gale, perhaps on a lee shore, to work the donkey engine and the schooner could be got underway by the crew of what would seem, compared with a square-rigger, to be a badly under-manned vessel. As schooners became larger and more masts were added, sails and gear increased in size and weight, and if it had not been for the steam donkey engine, these large vessels could not have been operated.

Part midship section of the four-masted schooner J W Clise *which was built at Ballard, Washington, in 1904. Her dimensions were 185.6ft x 41.0ft x 14.0ft and 715 tons net. Longitudinal strength was obtained by increasing the scantlings of the ceiling and by building up the keelson with additional logs. (Printed in Marine Review April 1909 by courtesy of the National Maritime Museum, San Francisco)*

The fore and main masts of the four-masted schooner Andy Mahony *sticking up out of a deck cargo of timber, which was held in place by the numerous chains passing across it. This West Coast vessel was built in 1902 at Aberdeen, Washington. This photograph illustrates how the big sails are secured to the gaff and boom. (Courtesy of the National Maritime Museum, San Francisco)*

The use of centreboards in four-masted schooners was a logical step from fitting them to three-masters where shallow draught hulls carried insufficient cargo and the narrower and deeper hulls without centreboards would not go about easily when in ballast. They were fitted to some of the largest four-masted schooners and to one five-master, the *Governor Ames*, a vessel 265ft long and 50ft beam. In the latter case, the centreboard was 35ft long and dropped 14ft. Centreboards did improve sailing qualities but took up valuable cargo space apart from leaking in older vessels, and they were generally discontinued in the 1890s. In harbours where vessels grounded at low water, they could prove disastrous and a great hazard, the boards getting jammed in the boxes by debris from the bottom.

Many of the three-masted schooners had been given moderately fine lines and were attractive, well-proportioned examples of the shipbuilder's art, whereas in the design of the four-, five- and six-masters which followed them, the natural grace of the smaller schooners was not continued in the long massive hulls with their wall sides, great sheer, high-steeved bowsprits and row of masts of equal height. The biggest schooners were built to shift the maximum amount of cargo possible under sail against the growing competition from barge traffic, and their immense size dominated everything.

Like all ship design, it was an individual matter and the expert could always recognize the work of a certain designer or shipbuilder, and Captain W J L Parker in *The Great Coal Schooners of New England* relates how the models made by three men – Albert Winslow, John L Frisbee and Crandall – 'represented the most practical in

This fine picture of the crew 'taking the line' aboard the Sophie Christenson – presumably a towing line – was possibly photographed from the tug after it had let go the hawser. The massive cathead in the foreground is seen end-on with the bowsprit shrouds or guys set up to it; the chain sheets from a jib lead down to the deck; and behind some of the crew is the fore staysail laced to a boom. She was built in 1901 at Port Blakely, Washington, of 570 tons. In 1913, the crew numbered eighteen. (Courtesy of the National Maritime Museum, San Francisco)

The Melrose *being towed down the Hoquiam River, Greys Harbour, Washington by the tug* Traveller, *her decks piled up with timber, and behind are the dark pine trees which supplied the wood. Of 542 tons, the* Melrose *was built on this river in 1902. Captain Klebingat was her master in the 1920s when she traded between San Francisco and some of the Pacific Islands.* (Courtesy of the National Maritime Museum, San Francisco)

big schooner design prior to 1890'. Albert Winslow, of Taunton, Maine, designed the hulls of many famous schooners over a period of about thirty years, and he did this by carving a half-model, a job which occupied him intermittently for between two and five weeks and for which he was usually paid $100. Of course he would have been given precise details by the yard manager or the shipowner regarding the type of hull required, what its carrying capacity was to be and perhaps what sort of performance was expected of the vessel at sea, but at the same time he was the designer and could either innovate a new hull-form or repeat an existing one. Whoever carved a half-model exerted great influence in a shipyard and the models hanging on the walls of the mould loft indicated the history of the yard and its fortunes. Albert Winslow had a keen eye for studying the model he had carved and checking it for the sweet flow of its lines. In 1888 he suggested that the very large four-masted schooner proposed by Captain Cornelius Davis, for which he had carved the half-model, be given a fifth mast. Thus was born the idea which resulted in the first five-masted schooner on the Atlantic coast, namely the *Governor Ames* of 1778 tons gross with dimensions of 245.6ft x 49.6ft x 21.2ft, built in the yard of Leavitt Storer at Waldoborough, Maine. The *List of Merchant Vessels of the United States* for 1890 gives the year of her building as 1889 and confirms that her official name was *Gov. Ames*, an abbreviation done to reduce telegraphic charges. This same publication listed six other *Gov.*'s and six spelled out in full.

The *Governor Ames* was a strongly-built vessel which was achieved partly as a result of her centreboard box and partly by running her hatch coamings in a continuous line from the foremost to the aftermost hatch. On her maiden passage she had

Left: Moored to a buoy at Brisbane in 1905 is the steel-hulled Kineo *during her round-the-world voyage, as described in the text. She was built in 1903 by A Sewall & Co of Bath, Maine, who were also her owners, and she measured 259.5ft x 45.3ft x 22.9ft, 2128 tons gross and 1867 tons net. Her troubles were certainly not over and she had to endure more vicissitudes before she reached home again.* (Courtesy of W J Lewis Parker)

the misfortune to be dismasted in December 1888, on the first night after sailing. The lanyards of her shrouds slackened in a strong SW gale, and although the crew tried to set them up again, the constant rolling of the schooner brought the foremast down and the other masts fell in quick succession. She anchored and was towed to Boston where she was re-rigged, and the deadeyes and lanyards were replaced with turnbuckles which gave no trouble for the rest of her life.

Another ten years were to elapse before the next five masted-schooner was launched which was the *Nathaniel T Palmer*. Altogether just under sixty were built on the East Coast in the years 1888-1920, and of these *Jane Palmer* was the largest

Below: This view of the Commerce, *built in 1900, depicts a vessel very similar in size and rig to the* Resolute *whose plans are given on page 141. Running with a quartering wind, the headsails, with the exception of the flying jib, are blanketed by the squaresail. The ringtail topsail is not set, but the vessel is making good speed.* (Courtesy of the National Maritime Museum, San Francisco)

at 3138 tons. Construction of her was begun in 1902 as a six-master with an auxiliary engine, to be named *Edward Burgess*; however, this was cancelled, the name changed and instead she was completed two years later as a pure sailing schooner.

In the design of big schooners, Albert Winslow was succeeded by men such as Fred W Rideout, Bowdoin B Crowninshield and John J Wardwell. The last-named hailed from Rockland, Maine, and designed at least 150 vessels, over eighty of which were constructed under his supervision at shipyards in Rockland and Stockton. It took him three or four days to carve the half-model and make the drawings of the first six-masted schooner to be built, namely the *George W Wells*, which H M Bean constructed in his yard at Camden, Maine. She was a fast schooner and in 1903 carried 4900 tons of coal from Philadelphia to Havana in 6 days 2 hours at an average speed of 13 knots.

To conceive the idea of building a schooner 300ft long was one thing, but to construct it was another when the material was wood. Vast amounts of timber were consumed by the enormous scantlings of the timbers required to prevent hogging and preserve the vessel's shape. The large five-masted schooner *Elizabeth Palmer* of 3065 tons gross and 2446 tons net register was constructed by Percy & Small at Bath, Maine, in 1903 with dimensions of 300.4ft x 48.3ft x 28.3ft and a capacity of 5000 tons of coal. Captain W J L Parker gives some indication of the prodigious sizes of material and gear required on this vessel in the pages of *The Great Coal Schooners of New England*. To give longitudinal strength, the keelson was composed of six tiers of 14in x 14in yellow pine logs with a sister keelson each side made up of three tiers of similar size; the ceiling was 13in x 14in yellow pine and the outer planking was 6in thick of the same wood; the frames, keel, stem and sternpost were of white oak; there was 120 fathoms of 2.5in chain on each of the two stockless anchors. When at sea in heavy weather the timbers creaked and groaned alarmingly to a young sailor, new to the sea, and many of them could move considerably under the stress of weather. The older schooners became badly strained and leaked continuously, which required the steam-powered pumps to be kept going permanently.

The four-masted schooner Huntley *in frame and ready for planking at Scott's Bay, Nova Scotia, in 1918. Of 520 tons, she had a length of 175.8ft. On ground covered with chips of wood, sawn timber has been laid out, and a pair of oxen are there to drag them to the sawpits or steam chest. (Public Archives, New Brunswick)*

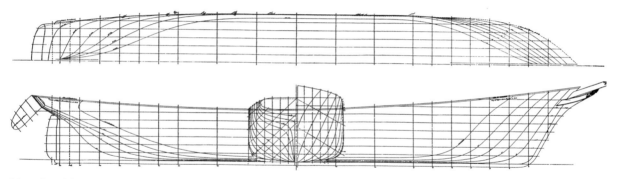

Lines plan of the five-masted schooner Margaret Haskell, *reproduced from plan prepared by B B Crowninshield for paper he read at the Society of Naval Architects & Engineers on 21 and 22 November 1907. Built in 1904 at Camden, Maine, by H M & R L Bean with dimensions of 252.3ft x 48.0ft x 20.5ft, 2114 tons gross and 1870 tons net, for Coastwise Transportation Co of Boston. Reproduced here with the assistance of the Douglas K and Linda J Lee Collection and by courtesy of W J Lewis Parker.*

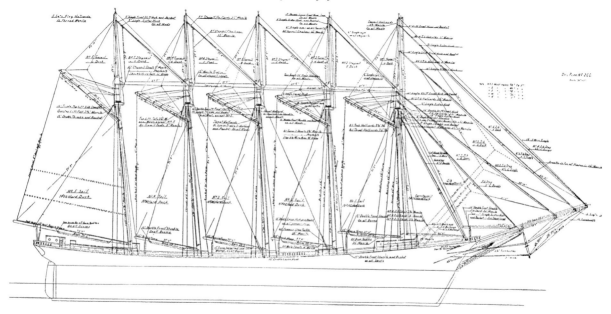

The big schooners had three decks, upper, main and lower. The main deck was usually composed only of beams with hatch coamings; the upper and lower decks were planked and had hatch coamings. The *Elizabeth Palmer* had a flush upper deck with four hatchways and three deckhouses, all of the latter being half-sunk into the deck and entered down companionways. The forward house was 28ft x 32ft and contained the foc's'le for the crew, engine room and cabin for the engineer; the midship house was abaft the mainmast and measured 20ft x 27ft and contained accommodation for the second mate and steward, the galley, mess-room and carpenter's shop; the after house measured 30ft x 32ft and contained the master's cabin with all home comforts, the main saloon with oak and cherry panelling and heavy leather furniture, two or three staterooms, an owner's cabin, bathroom, dining saloon, mate's cabin and pantry. All the accommodation both fore and aft, was steam-heated by the donkey boiler.

Steam-powered winches were used to hoist the sails, which were made of the heaviest cloth obtainable. On a similar Palmer schooner, the lower masts were of Oregon pine and measured 122ft in length and approximately 30in thick at the

Sail and rigging plan of the five-masted schooner Margaret Haskell, *from the same sources as detailed in the lines plan above. This is a unique drawing of a type rarely to be found; it details the length of spars, the quality of canvas of the sails and the sizes of rigging. The assistance of the Douglas K and Linda J Lee Collection and courtesy of W J Lewis Parker is gratefully acknowledged.*

partners; the topmasts were 60ft long, the spanker boom was 81ft and the other four booms were 49ft. The standing rigging was of wire set up with rigging screws. The crew would number eleven to fourteen all told in the five- and six-masted vessels; even the seven-masted *Thomas W Lawson* only carried sixteen all told. In the early 1880s, a seaman was paid $16 to $18 per month but after 1892 the International Seamen's Union forced up the rates so that $25 per month was a minimum and by 1902, $35 per month was demanded. (The exchange rate for dollars into sterling was still about $5 = £1.) The cost of building the all-wood schooners varied from $40 to $50 per gross ton.

Coal was loaded at Philadelphia, Baltimore, Newport News and Norfolk for New

Launch of the Baker Palmer *in 1901 from the yard of G L Weldt at Waldoboro, Maine. This white-hulled three-decked schooner, constructed for the Boston fleet of W F Palmer, had a net tonnage of 2240 and dimensions of 284.9ft x 46.5ft x 21.9ft. (Courtesy of Peabody Museum of Salem)*

York and Boston; other schooners might be carrying lumber from Maine or hard pine from the Southern States, which meant first filling the holds and then stacking the timber on the decks high above the bulwarks, leaving deep narrow wells around the masts for the crew to scramble down to the gear belayed on the fife rails, unless makeshift fiferails were rigged on top of the deck cargo. A few schooners made ambitious voyages around Cape Horn and into the Pacific while others went to Australia, China or Europe. The *Governor Ames* was one of these. Captain Davis took her to San Francisco in 1890-91 in the search for higher freights and thereafter worked in the coastal trade followed by a voyage to Port Pirie in Australia returning via Honolulu. After another year carrying lumber she sailed for Liverpool which she reached in June 1894 after a passage of 139 days from Port Blakely. Two months later she was back on the East Coast of America after an absence of four years. During these

Deck scene aboard the four-masted schooner Albert D Cummins *looking forward from the poop with the sea breaking over the port bulwarks. She was not constructed until 1920 by the Beaumont Shipbuilding Co at Beaumont, Texas, with a length of 189.5ft and a gross tonnage of 1163. She survived until 1947 when she was burned for scrap at Philadelphia. Copied from postcard in MacGregor Collection. Message on the reverse reads as follows:*

The 4 m. American Schooner "Albert D. Cummins" of Philadelphia, at sea. Even in comparatively fine weather she ships water over both rails, & in heavy weather the main deck becomes a seething mass. It was from the near rigging in the picture that I was washed away from the mizen [sic] halyards three times one night, whilst trying to lower the sail during that gale. [signed] Chappie.
Taken from the poop in the North Sea [dated] Sept 1920

This must have been on her maiden voyage. (MacGregor Collection)

This well-known view of the Edward B Winslow *is one of the few shots ever taken of a deeply-laden schooner under full sail plunging through the seas in a strong wind. This huge vessel measured 318.4ft x 50.0ft x 23.7ft, which was only 1.8ft shorter and 0.2ft narrower than the six-masted Schooner* Edward J Lawrence *built the same year. Both had an identical breadth and were built for the same owner, J S Winslow of Portland, Maine, and so were possibly sisters.* (Courtesy of the Peabody Museum of Salem)

long passages she found that a pure gaff rig was largely unsuitable for the big swells and heavy seas to be found in the open oceans.

However, nothing daunted by the terrible punishment she suffered, the Bath firm of Arthur Sewall & Co despatched their latest five-masted schooner, the steel-hulled *Kineo*, to Manila in January 1905 with 2707 tons of coal for the Navy's use. Recalling the hardships meted out to the *Governor Ames* in rounding Cape Horn, the *Kineo* sailed out via the Cape of Good Hope, which was the regular route taken by square-rigged ships for decades. Writing in the *National*

Left: Aboard the five-masted schooner H K Hall *at the time of her launch in 1902 are her builder, Henry K Hall, and his son, James W Hall. She registered 1105 tons net. See page 140 for picture of her before launching.* (Courtesy of the National Maritime Museum, San Francisco)

Below: Interior of the saloon aboard the West Coast four-masted schooner Blakeley. (Courtesy of the National Maritime Museum, San Francisco)

Shipping a sea abreast of the main rigging on the port side of the four-masted schooner Henry S Little *which specialised in the coal, ice and phosphate trades. She was fitted with centreboards like many of her kind, having been built in 1889 at Bath, Maine, of 1096 tons gross.* (Courtesy of W J Lewis Parker)

Fisherman (*c*1981), F F Kaiser describes the problems caused by the weather to the *Kineo*. After leaving Norfolk, Virginia, she quickly experienced the sort of problems that were to dog her world-wide voyaging, because soon after passing Cape Henry a westerly gale badly damaged the foresail and mainsail, as well as the ship's boat slung over the stern. The master, Frank W Patten, an experienced captain of a square-rigger, found the constant rolling of the schooner unnerving and longed for square canvas to keep the vessel more steady. When there was little or no wind, the sails slatted so heavily back and forwards that the jaws of the gaffs and booms started to break, and so it was found that the wisest course was to lower the big gaff sails and wait for some wind to blow. When running the easting down in the South Atlantic and southern Indian Ocean, it was often necessary to lower the gaff sails to save the gear. Square-riggers would have been running before these winds and even a barquentine would have had enough square canvas aloft to perform better. With heavy seas breaking over the rail and sweeping across her long open deck, it was found impossible to reef her gaff sails in heavy weather, which resulted in the crew having to perform this task in advance of expected bad weather, thus losing speed when the wind was light.

There was a good supply of coal aboard for the steam donkey engine but providing sufficient supplies of fresh water for the boiler was a constant problem. When it rained, some schooners used to close all the scuppers and save the water for use in the boiler. After discharging the coal at Manila, the barnacle and weed-encrusted *Kineo* headed towards Newcastle, New South Wales, to load more cargo, but progress was very slow and a typhoon tore the sails, wrecked the stern boat again and flooded the cabin, ruining the stores and fresh vegetables. In addition everyone aboard was stricken with beriberi and became incapable of working. With immense difficulty they made Brisbane, about two months or more after leaving Manila; the master and a few of the crew could just manage to crawl about. The authorities removed everyone from the vessel to let them recover.

Aboard the five-masted schooner Edna Hoyt, *the crew are lifting off the hatch beams – 'strong-backs' in America – preparatory to unloading the cargo. This vessel was built in 1920 at Thomaston, Maine, with a beam of 41ft. (MacGregor Collection)*

Riding high in ballast, the steel-hulled Thomas W Lawson *is under full sail with all her topsails and staysails set, and the shadows cast on the sails make fascinating patterns. Her appearance is greatly improved if a piece of paper is laid lengthwise along the hull at an imaginary load waterline level. (Courtesy of Peabody Museum of Salem)*

Five weeks later, the schooner sailed south to Newcastle and loaded coal for Hawaii which was safely reached. Here she loaded over 3000 tons of sugar and sailed for Philadelphia around Cape Horn in the depths of winter with the prospect of having to surmount the serious problems already experienced when running the easting down, earlier in the voyage. At least the master knew what to expect in his deeply-laden schooner, although the new crew shipped in Newcastle probably did not. However, she rounded the Horn but found severe weather in the South Atlantic, with big seas sweeping across her open deck and making work impossible. To make matters worse, steam could not be raised as the boiler tubes gave out and all the work had to done by hand; this was particularly hard on a crew grown accus-

In a light breeze, the Edward J Lawrence *is running 'wing and wing' with the sails on the spanker mast boomed out to port to catch some more wind. The figure-of-eight shape, laid on its side, taken up by most hulls is well illustrated in this picture. Her owners, J S Winslow & Co, owned twenty-one vessels in 1913 of which no less than five were six-masted schooners; they also managed the Palmer fleet consisting of twelve magnificent large schooners. (Courtesy of the Mariners Museum, Newport News)*

tomed to a donkey engine. By the end of the voyage, which occupied 205 days, there was not a mast hoop left and the sails were held to the masts by lengths of wire. Captain Patten made sure not to go on ocean voyages again in a schooner, and Sewall's likewise abandoned the projects they had long contemplated of sending schooners out on world-wide trade routes. The *Kineo* had two diesel engines installed in 1911 and, after being cut down to a petrol-carrying barge, she was sold to Brazil in 1947 and disappeared from the register in 1969.

The peak years for building multi-masted schooners, prior to the First World War, were 1898-1908. Included in this period was the introduction of all the ten six-masted schooners ever launched and also of the only seven-master. Howard I Chapelle considered that these huge schooners were awkward to handle in confined waters and, because of their deficiency in longitudinal strength, could not be sailed really hard without becoming strained. The sheer size of the huge gaff sails made them very difficult to reef with such small crews, in spite of the invaluable donkey engine, and skippers had to gauge weather conditions carefully. Very few schooners on the East Coast were built of steel, largely because of cost, but important exceptions were the *Kineo* with five masts, the six-master *William L Douglas* and the *Thomas W Lawson*.

As regards schooners with more than three masts built on the West Coast, by far the earliest to be rigged with four masts was the ex-barge *Victoria* which in 1864 was rebuilt as a schooner of 344 tons at San Francisco. Next in date comes the *Novelty* in 1886, but she was given four pole masts on a steamer's hull. The following year there were three proper schooners, the *Kitsap*, *Volunteer* and *Wm F Vitzemann*. For the rest of the century, sizes of four-masters were generally in the 550-750 tons range and the first of over 1000 tons, the *Rosamund*, did not appear until 1900. The first five-masted schooner was the *Louis* of 1888 and 831 tons, but she had a steamer's hull; the first five-master built as a real schooner was the *Inca* of 1014 tons, built in 1896 at Port Blakely, Washington. In his book *The History of American Sailing Ships*, Howard I Chapelle gives plans of the *Inca* showing a broad shallow draught hull with slight deadrise and rounded bilges. The waterlines and diagonals are superimposed in the plan, but the entrance and run are convex with some hollow in the lower body in the run. There is a big sheer with the hull swept forward at the bow; the bowsprit and jibboom are not too long and support four headsails, with the fore staysail set on a boom; there is no yard on the foremast; the spanker mast is drawn with a large gaff sail and jib-headed topsail above, but a leg-of-mutton sail is indicated by a dotted line.

On the Pacific coast, 130 four-masted schooners were constructed in the years 1887 to 1904; of the five-masters, only nine were built between 1888 and 1916 (inclusive). None of these vessels were fitted with centreboards. A yard was generally carried on the foremast for a square sail set below it and triangular raffees above, and these were set on the windward side when the wind was abaft the beam. The late John Lyman contributed a valuable paper on the *Sailing Vessels of the Pacific Coast and their Builders* which the Marine Research Society of San Diego published as a bulletin subsequently to 1941.

A single yard was also carried at one time by many of the East Coast three- and

From the bowsprit looking aft aboard the six-masted schooner Edward B Winslow. *On top of the forward deckhouse is the massive black-painted exhaust of the donkey engine which drove the halyard winches, pumps, windlass and cargo winches. The unbroken upper deck stretches away into the distance.* (Courtesy of Peabody Museum of Salem)

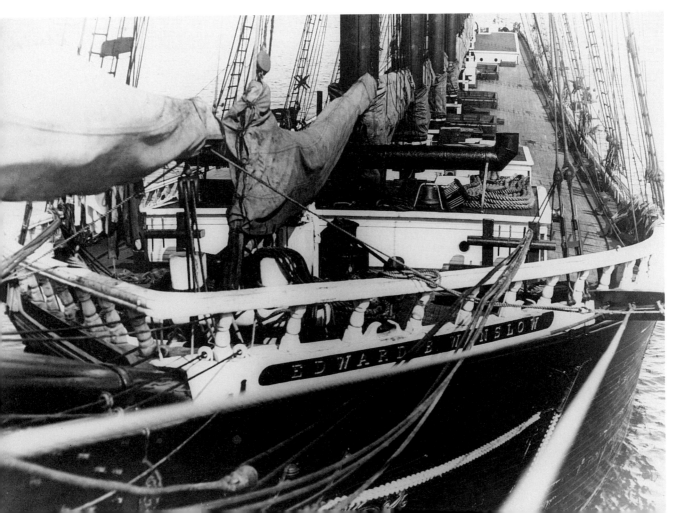

four-masted schooners. The square sail was not bent to the yard in the usual way but was secured to hoops which could be hauled out or in, and when furled it hung vertically from the yard on the foreside of the mast. However, the yards disappeared about 1890, although B B Crowninshield commented in *Fore-and-Afters*, 'just why I don't quite understand', and he continued, 'perhaps it was for the same reason that the topmast staysails between the masts on the big schooners were seldom renewed when worn out. All new vessels had them with their first set of sails but when they were gone they were rarely replaced; the saying was that they were "not worth their keep".'

The following comments, which were published in the American East Coast magazine *The Rudder* (Vol XIII, June 1902), give an uncompromising critique on the design of East-Coast versus West-Coast schooners. The editor was Thomas Fleming Day, and as no author's name was given with this piece, it may have been written by him.

The George W Wells *was the first American six-master to be built. She was launched in 1900 and was of 2970 tons gross and had a length of 319.3ft. Some idea of the massive qualities of her enormous hull can be gained by studying the three levels of staging rigged along her sides, and the numbers of shipyard workers caulking her seams.* (Courtesy of Peabody Museum of Salem)

The coasting vessel of to-day on our eastern seaboard is degenerate. Its decadence is the result of greed. The constant cry of the schooner owner for the last two or three decades has been capacity. For increased cargo space he is willing to sacrifice everything else. The craft turned out to-day are simply sailing barges, unweatherly and bad sea boats. There was a time and there were schooners that did and could go to windward in any kind of weather in which sail could be carried, but with few exceptions these vessels have passed away, and the ones that have taken their place are huge, unhandy hulks that make foul weather of all but moderate and favoring winds. While these boats carry enormous cargoes for their keel lengths,

Looking aloft on the six-masted schooner Mertie B Crowley, *built in 1907 and of 2824 tons. On looking at this photograph, Emmett A Hoskins remarked: 'You can tell right away it's an East Coast schooner; there are no jigs [ie no tackles] on the halyards. Everything is hoisted by steam'. The topping lifts go to a double block shackled to the starboard trestletree. The jib-headed topsails are hooped to the masts like gaff sails.* (Courtesy of the National Maritime Museum, San Francisco)

they are slow in making a passage, and in bad weather cannot be forced to windward. Days and days are lost through their unhandiness, especially in crowded roadsteds, where they have frequently to wait owing to their inability to work clear of the surrounding craft.

Again, if they are caught in a blow, they either have to anchor or run back to shelter. Many times during the winter they are driven off shore and obliged to lie-to for days, not being able to carry sail enough to work inshore and employ the lee to make up for their port. Nor is this the worst. Both light and loaded when in a seaway they will not tack, and many of them refuse to wear unless stripped of their after sail. Very few of them are properly hung, steering hard, and obliging the flatting of the head sheets, thus deadening their way. While admitting that the problem of designing this type of vessel is an exceedingly difficult one, owing to the change of load, there is no reason why our naval architects could not design a better class of craft than those turned out to-day by the rule-of-thumb builders. A vessel carrying less cargo per foot of length, properly modeled, could be built that would sail all around the present craft, and by making quicker and more reliable passages earn just as much money as the slow-sailing coasters of to-day.

The vessel whose lines we give is one built on the Pacific coast, and is a much better modeled craft than our average eastern vessel. From what I have seen of the west-coast vessels, I have no hesitancy in saying that they are very superior to those employed on our seaboard. Of course the conditions are somewhat different, but the western builder has not relapsed into the barge idea and still tries to give his vessel a ship-like shape. The rig shown on the *Resolute* is certainly more handy than ours, the use of the jib-headed spanker and ring-topsail making the shortening of the after-canvas an easy job.

The *Resolute* was designed by George H. Hitchings and built by Hitchings and Joyce, at Hoguiam, Washington. She is designed to carry 800,000 feet of lumber. Her loading dimensions are: load water line, 172 feet; breadth extreme, 39 feet 6 inches; depth of hold, 14 feet [see page 141 for lines plan].

After the appearance of the first six-masted schooners, vessels carrying seven or eight masts were being mentioned, and several authorities were quoted at the time. The *Nautical Gazette* of December 1900 contained a proposal to build an eight-master of steel with dimensions of 400ft x 52ft x 30ft. The following year, inspired by such talk or by the enthusiasm which his six-masted schooner, *George W Wells*, engendered in the public, her managing owner, Captain John G Crowley, commissioned Bowdoin B Crowninshield to design a seven-masted schooner to be built of steel. This monster vessel was built by the Fore River Ship & Engine Building Co at Quincy, Massachusetts, at a cost of $240,000 and launched in July 1902 with the name of *Thomas W Lawson*. Her measurements were 375.6ft x 50.0ft x 22.9ft and tonnages of 5218 gross and 4914 net register; she had a double bottom to contain water ballast which amounted to a total of 1069 tons and this brought her down to a draught of 12ft which made her stiff enough to carry sail. When loaded with 9200 tons of coal she drew 29ft 10in. She had two complete steel decks and the windlass was under the topgallant foc's'le; the foremast was 33in diameter but the other six masts were 30in.

On her maiden passage from Boston to Philadelphia in ballast, she was going along well in a light SE breeze when it became necessary to go about. Her designer, Crowninshield, was aboard and recounts the episode: 'I asked the skipper how long it would take to tack; his reply was, "Well! You go below and eat your dinner, and when you come on deck she may be off on the other tack." My dinner was postponed and she did "come in stays" and gathered way on the port tack in about ten minutes. The order was given: "Stand by to tack" – "Ready about" – Hard a-lee", and as the wheel was put down the head sheets were slacked up and at the same time the after boom was hauled to weather as she came into the wind . . .' and she slowly came round. But the following morning off Cape Cod she would not go about and they had to wear her. However, when loaded, she handled like a yacht.

The *Thomas W Lawson* carried coal under sail on coastal trips for a short time, but when freight rates fell, her topmasts were sent down and she was towed between Texas and Philadelphia carrying oil. Then in November 1907 she was chartered to carry case oil across the Atlantic to London under sail, and on reaching the Scilly Isles six weeks later, she anchored in the open sea to ride out a gale, but her anchor chains parted and she was driven ashore. The master and engineer were the only survivors.

During a period of ten years, 1900-09, ten six-masted schooners were built in the United States on the Atlantic Coast, but it should be noted that the first of these, the *George W Wells*, was not the first six-master to be built because the iron screw steamer *Great Britain* was officially registered as a schooner with six masts away back in 1844. The largest of these six-masters was the *Wyoming* built in 1909, and it is worth comparing her size with that of the huge American clipper *Great Republic*, as first built, and also listing the dimensions of the ss *Great Britain*:

Two of the crew working aloft on the crosstrees aboard the four-masted schooner Copperfield, *which which was built in 1919 at Chickasaw, Alabama, and owned at Mobile in the same State. She was of 691 tons gross and had a length of 172.5ft; she survived until 1932 when she was lost off the Jamaican coast.*
(MacGregor Collection)

NAME	YEAR	DIMENSIONS	DISPLACEMENT
Great Republic	1853	335.0ft x 53.0ft x 38.0ft	4455 tons (USA o.m.)
Wyoming	1909	329.5ft x 50.1ft x 30.4ft	3036 tons net
			3730 tons gross
ss *Great Britain*	1843	274.0ft x 48.2ft x 31.5ft	1795 tons net
			3270 tons gross

The six-masted schooners built on the Atlantic coast in order of launching:

NAME	YEAR	TONS GROSS	WHERE BUILT	BUILDER	MATERIAL
George W Wells	1900	2970	Camden, Maine	H M Bean	wood
Eleanor A Percy	1900	3402	Bath, Maine	Percy & Small	wood
Addie M Lawrence	1902	2807	Bath, Maine	Percy & Small	wood
William L Douglas	1903	3708	Quincy, Mass	Fore River SB Co	steel
Ruth E Merrill	1904	3003	Bath, Maine	Percy & Small	wood
Alice M Lawrence	1906	3132	Bath, Maine	Percy & Small	wood
Mertie B Crowley	1907	2824	Rockland, Maine	Cobb, Butler Co	wood
Edward J Lawrence	1908	3350	Bath, Maine	Percy & Small	wood
Edward B Winslow	1908	3424	Bath, Maine	Percy & Small	wood
Wyoming	1909	3730	Bath, Maine	Percy & Small	wood

This list appeared in *Log Chips* in July 1948 (Vol I).

The last six-masted schooner afloat was the *Edward J Lawrence* which was burned at Portland, Maine, on 27 December 1925, so that this breed lasted a mere twenty-five years.

There was a great boom in the second half of the First World War for building schooners owing to the shortage of tonnage, and in the years 1917-20, on the East Coast of the United States there were constructed ten five-masters, 133 four-masters and many large three-masters.

By contrast, Pacific coast shipyards launched twenty-two five-masted schooners in 1917 and fifty-seven in 1918, according to John Lyman's lists. Of the four-masters, forty-one were built in these two years. Prior to the entry of America into the War in 1917, Norwegian owners had been ordering schooners; later the United States only allowed her Allies to order, and forty auxiliary steam schooners were built in Oregon and Washington in 1918 for the French Government. Most had short lives of only a few years and many were laid up in France.

In the Maritime Provinces of Canada, approximately thirty-five four-masted schooners were built in the years 1917–20; five of these were auxiliaries and three of the total were of over 1000 tons gross.

The five-master Dorothy Palmer, *built by the same shipyard two years after the* Baker Palmer, *accompanied by a twin-funnelled tug in this* contre jour *photograph.* (MacGregor Collection)

Other vessels to be given six masts in the United States and rigged with fore-and-aft sails were the oil barge *Navahoe*, built in 1908 of 7718 tons, but always towed; the *Dovrefjeld* which was converted in 1917 from the PS *Rhode Island*; the *Katherine*, ex-*County of Linlithgow* (1887, 4m ship, 2296 tons) was converted into an auxiliary schooner in 1919; and in 1920 three steamers were converted to the rig of six-masted schooner, namely, the *Oregon Fir* and *Oregon Pine* (both 2526 tons of wood), and the *Fort Laramie* with a Ferris-type hull. Conversions during the Second World War are described in Chapter 18.

Schooners Around the World | *15*

DUE TO American influence, the West Indies had a long tradition of building and operating schooners and the nature of the islands encouraged schooner traffic until recent times. As bases for privateers and pirates, the West Indies were ideal and reference has already been made to them on several occasions. Between the two World Wars, the schooners became run-down and few new ones were built, but the creation of the Schooner Pool Authority in the British West Indies in 1942 stabilised things by making work available and organising freights. The schooners had been entirely fore-and-aft rigged for some years, and were mostly two-masters with a sprinkling of three-masters. In 1921, a four-master of 696 tons, the *Marie J Thompson* was built in the Bahamas, presumably because of the high freight rates, but the postwar boom was virtually over by then.

For Australia, the British Admiralty had designed a schooner in 1802 for use at Sydney, and schooners were in use as coastal and inter-island traders in the nineteenth and twentieth centuries. There was always a big fleet sailing to and from

The American schooner Wanderer *at Shanghai c1865-70 drying her sails at anchor. She belonged to Augustine Heard & Co, the China merchants, but it is not known what her trade was.* (Courtesy of Peabody Museum of Salem)

Above: Presumably this vessel is Pilot Cutter No 1 at anchor in some hot climate with her sails neatly furled. Perhaps this is the River Hooghly. Among the square-rigged ships at anchor in the distance can be made out, between the schooner's masts, the famous clipper The Tweed. (MacGregor Collection)

Below: Drying her sails in Sydney Harbour is the schooner Federal *which was built at Balmain, NSW, in 1900 and registered 96 tons. The fore square sail appears to be bent to the lower yard. The hulls of many schooners in both Australia and New Zealand were painted white.* (MacGregor Collection)

Left: The fore-and-aft schooner Rahra, *built at Lake Macquarie, NSW, in 1912. She originally traded between Melbourne and Hobart and by 1924 had had an auxiliary 40hp engine fitted; she then registered 93 tons gross with dimensions of 93.5ft x 23.0ft x 6.8ft. About this time she worked the Ellice and Tokelau Islands, which lie 5° to 10° south of the Equator, for Carruthers & Hedstrom.* (MacGregor Collection)

Below: Lines, deck layout, sail and rigging plan for 'Schooner for Port Jackson' redrawn by the author and Paul Roberts from Admiralty draughts at National Maritime Museum, Greenwich. Plans dated 1803 sent to Port Jackson, Australia – now called Sydney – for vessel to be constructed there. No spar dimensions listed on plans, so these were reconstructed from John Fincham's Masting Ships *(1829) as for a 'common schooner'; contemporary text books on rigging and sailmaking also consulted. Dimensions: 53ft 0in (on deck) x 17ft 6in (extreme) x 8ft 0in and 68 tons.*

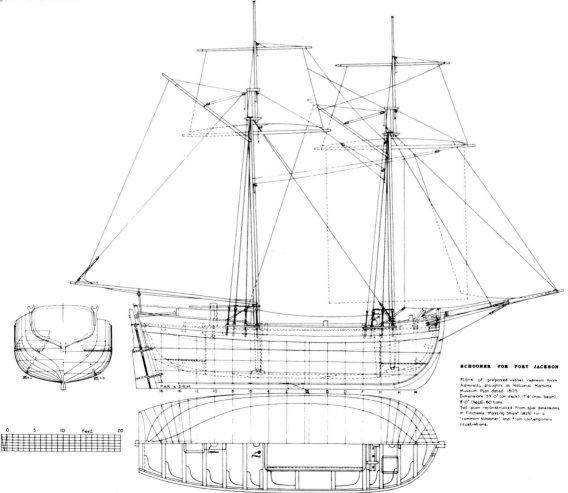

SCHOONER FOR PORT JACKSON

Plans of proposed vessel, redrawn from Admiralty draughts at National Maritime Museum. Plan dated 1803
Dimensions: 53' 0" (on deck), 17' 6" (max. beam), 8' 0" (hold). 60 tons
Sail plan reconstructed from spar dimensions in Fincham's "Masting Ships" (1829) for a "common schooner" and from contemporary illustrations.

Above: A pearling 'lugger' under sail off Australia's north-west coast with a Broome registration number on her bows. The masts seem of about equal height, there is no forestay to the stem and a large jib is the only headsail. The average size of these schooners was 45ft to 65ft. By c1970 or so they all had auxiliary engines and were ketch-rigged. Back in the 1880s they were lug-rigged and had the mizen hauled out to a boom or bumpkin; at that date, the mizen was barely shorter than the mainmast. (Courtesy of E K Patterson)

Above right: This fine photograph shows the New Zealand topsail schooner Huia *under sail. She was built in 1894 at Aratapu in Kaipara Harbour in North Aucland, by James Barbour who carved a model of her; no plans were drawn. She measured 204 tons gross, 115.1ft long and 25.2ft beam. Her life was spent trading to and from Australia, around New Zealand and Pacific islands. She went ashore on a reef off the southern tip of New Caledonia in 1951.* (Collection of the late Cyril L Hume)

Below: Three local schooners at Mahé in the Seychelle Islands, probably off the Long Pier at Port Victoria, with the rocky peaks behind. Sugar, tobacco and spices were exported in the nineteenth century. It is interesting to note the different rigs. (Neptune Publications)

Tasmania, and one of the last three-masted topsail schooners registered at Hobart was the *Alma Doepel*, built in 1903 but eventually cut down to a motor vessel.

Around New Zealand, schooners were in common use and Clifford Hawkins has recounted much of their history in the Auckland Province. Many fore-and-aft rigged schooners and some topsail schooners were built to serve the isolated communities and to trade with many of the Pacific Islands. Some were lofty vessels with topgallant yards, and the regattas for commercial craft made imposing sights around the turn of the century.

The first scow or flat-bottomed barge with chines to be constructed in New Zealand was the *Lake Erie* built in 1873, and by 1900 scows were very popular. Cargo was carried on deck as the hull was only 5ft deep, but centreboards were employed to make the hulls sail better to windward. Two- and three-masted scows were constructed in addition to ketches, and the three-masters *Zingara* and *Pirate* had square topsails. Although sterns were square, the bows were often pointed with raking stems and they certainly carried bowsprits. The *Rangi* was the last scow without auxiliary power and she continued to work under sail into the 1930s.

Island schooners at Bequia in the Windward Islands. Their fore topmasts have been removed and the vessel on the right has been hove down to inspect her bottom. (Courtesy of R A Calvert)

An unidentified schooner flying a pale blue flag bearing a white crescent moon which is probably Turkish. Painted in watercolour by R H Nibbs, it dates from c1815-45. The foremast is stepped very far forward and the fore yard is placed some distance below the hounds, requiring a deep roach to the foot of the topsail to clear the stays. (Private collection)

White-hulled fore-and-aft schooners, with three or two masts, lie in the harbour of Georgetown, Barbados. (MacGregor Collection)

Pilot Boats and Fishermen |

IN THE British Isles, pilot boats were rigged as fore-and-aft schooners at several places such as Fleetwood, Swansea and Liverpool. At Liverpool, the first of this rig was the *Pioneer* No 6 of 53 tons built in 1852, and altogether there were sixteen schooners, the last being the clipper-bowed *George Holt* No 10, built in 1892 and sold in 1904. In *The Way of the World at Sea* (1896), W J Gordon writes:

> These Liverpool boats are reputed to be among the best afloat. They are good-sized schooners, averaging about seventy tons, fast and weatherly, and able to keep the sea in all weathers. And it is very rough outside the Mersey bar on some occasions.

The Swansea pilot boats were smaller than these, probably being developed from a shallop, and they had a very raking mainmast. In the 1790s the schooners

Many of the pilot schooners on the East Coast of the United States were splendid vessels with large suits of sails, somewhat similar to the bigger fishing schooners. This one, the Adams, *was built at Essex, Massachusetts, in 1889 and was photographed by N L Stebbins in 1891. She looked similar to* Hesper *No 5. (Courtesy of the Peabody Museum of Salem)*

165

were small in size, measuring 21ft long and 6.5ft beam, but they were built larger from about 1860 and were then decked over; by 1898 there were only two still in use. On the Continent, the pilot schooners at Dunkirk and Bremerhaven resembled the Liverpool boats.

The Virginia pilot boat model has already been described and schooner rig was the recognised one for American pilot boats. In the 1880s there were thirty schooners based on New York and they carried pilots as much as 600 miles out to sea in the search for ships. Many pilot boats had vertical stems and were influenced

Sail plan and rigging details of the New York pilot schooner Phantom *which was designed by D J Lawlor and built in East Boston in 1868 with dimensions of 76ft-4in (overall) x 19ft-8in x 19ft-8in (draft aft). As the fore topmast was only a light spar for displaying flags, neither flying jib nor gaff topsail could be carried, unlike the schooners of the 1890s. It seems odd that only two shrouds are fitted to the foremast and but a single one to the main, whereas the* Adams *of 1889 (page 165) had three shrouds on each mast. Plan drawn by George F Campbell.* (Courtesy of Model Expo Inc, Mt Pocono, Pennsylvania)

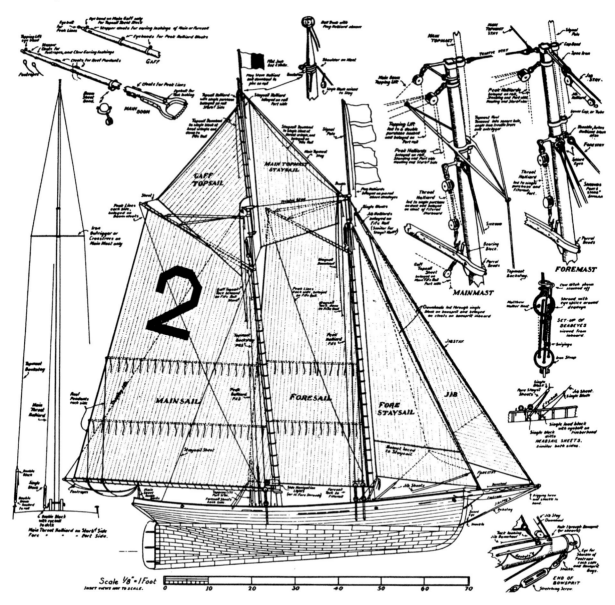

The Mersey *on the stocks in 1875 in the yard of William Thomas at Amlwch, Anglesey. She was constructed for the Liverpool pilotage service and measured 80.7ft x 19.0ft x 10.8ft and 79 tons. (W Stewart Rees)*

by the fishing schooner as to rig but often discarded the fore topmast and so only carried two headsails.

The chebacco boats used for fishing off New England, as described in Chapter 4, were not large enough for the expanding fishing industry and the pinkies were not fast enough. To overcome these problems, ports such as Essex and Gloucester began building 45-ton finer-lined schooners in the late 1830s, and fishing was by

A Dunkirk pilot schooner at anchor with four pilots returning to the shore station. The fore staysail is set on a boom, the foremast is a pole but the mainmast has a fidded topmast. Copied from a postcard printed in blue. (MacGregor Collection)

Right: The British fishing schooner Spirit, *built by James Hood at Sandwich, Kent, in 1851 to the order of Robert Huntley, contained a wet well divided into three sections with 6in long slots in the planking to induce the water to move freely in and out. Four months of the year were to be spent carrying live eels from Ireland to market; for the remainder of the year she was to be in the Iceland cod fishery. Her measurements were 74ft length of keel, 18ft breadth, 10ft depth of hold, 22ft length of well, and 116 tons n.m. The engraving indicates a schooner intended to race fish to the market.* (Engraving in *Illustrated London News* 9 August 1851 p.204)

Below: Photographed at Bridgwater by W A Sharman, the King's Oak *is dried out and has staging hung over her sides for work to her planking. This schooner was built by Fellows at Great Yarmouth in 1884 as a fishing ketch. This photograph shows that she had fine lines with a bilge keel. During 1891-92 she was lengthened by 15ft so that she measured 88.2ft x 19.5ft x 9.4ft, 82 tons gross and was then re-rigged as a schooner.* Lloyd's Register *1892 is the first year in which she appears as a schooner with the entry 'for fishing purposes'; by 1893 her new owners, Spillers & Bakers, had transferred her from Yarmouth to Cardiff. By c1908, Richard Harris of Watchet was the owner and* Lloyd's *still classed her as a schooner 'for fishing purposes'; 1924 was the last year they listed her. If the entry remained correct all those years, she must have been almost unique in British waters.* (MacGregor Collection)

The sails of the fishing schooner
Vigilant *hang listless in the
calm air. This type of fishing
boat was in use in the middle
of last century off the coast of
New England. A staysail could
be set from the main topmast.*
(Courtesy of the Peabody
Museum of Salem)

hand lines from the schooner's deck. Gradually larger boats evolved which resulted in the 'clipper' types of the late 1850s, an example of which was the *Flying Fish* of 1857 with an overall length of 74ft, a beam of 21ft, and a hull having a long straight keel, hollow lines and a clipper bow.

The yacht designer, Edward Burgess, introduced greater depth of hull and steeper deadrise into the *Carrie E Phillips* in 1886, making her a big craft of 110 tons. The curved stem introduced by T F McManus about 1900 became known as an 'Indian head' and was adopted by the entire Gloucester fleet. The 'knockabout' schooners of this period had no bowsprits but instead possessed a longer and finely modelled hull.

A cup was donated in 1910 for the winner of the annual schooner races to be held at Digby, Nova Scotia, and this helped to promote continued interest in the schooners. Halifax and Lunenberg also built and owned many fishing schooners, and it was at the latter port that the celebrated *Bluenose* was launched in 1920. Racing continued throughout the 1930s until the final one in 1938. A replica *Bluenose* was built in 1963.

Ships of many nationalities fished on the Grand Banks off Newfoundland and not least of these were the Portugese who continued to send large schooners across the Atlantic even after the Second World War. Before the War, in 1936, the fleet had numbered fifty-seven of which only twenty were auxiliaries; there were also some two-masted topsail schooners. Thirty years later the fleet had shrunk to one barquentine, six four-masted schooners and two three-masted schooners, and although not all of them had bowsprits, at least they all had gaff sails and some even had fidded topmasts; in addition, they all had powerful auxiliary engines. It was in the year 1950 that Alan Villiers sailed aboard the Portuguese four-masted schooner *Argus* and immortalised her in his subsequent account of the voyage. In that year, apart from the trawlers and motor ships, there were thirty-one schooners, two of which had no engines at all, and one barquentine. The steel-hulled *Argus* of 696 tons was built in Holland in 1938 and carried fifty-three dorymen.

Schooners seem to have been rarely used in the British Isles for fishing, although the *Illustrated London News* reproduced an engraving in August 1851 of the *Spirit* of 116 tons which was constructed with three wet wells for carrying eels from Ireland and cod from Iceland. She had a straight stem and a lofty fore-and-aft rig. Another type, according to Roy Clark in *The Longshoremen*, was the Irish wherry which varied in size from 20 to 50 tons and was employed at Skerries, just north of Dublin, in the first half of the nineteenth century. In appearance they resembled the Swansea pilot schooners with a straight stem, vertical foremast and markedly raked mainmast, but they had longer gaffs. The photograph on page 168 shows a schooner-rigged fishing schooner called *King's Oak* which was converted to this rig when she was lengthened in the 1890s. With her masts so closely spaced, she looks more like a clipper schooner that had survived from thirty years previously, and with her long hollow run and large mainsail she must have been a fast vessel.

A rigged whole-hull model of the Benjamin W Latham. *She was built in 1902 at Essex, Massachusetts, and began her life as a mackerel seiner out of Noank, Connecticut; she lasted until 1943. Her shape of bow was termed an 'Indian header'. The schooner* L A Dunton, *preserved at Mystic Seaport, provides an example of one of these fishing boats.* (Courtesy of Model Expo Inc, Mt Pocono, Pennsylvania)

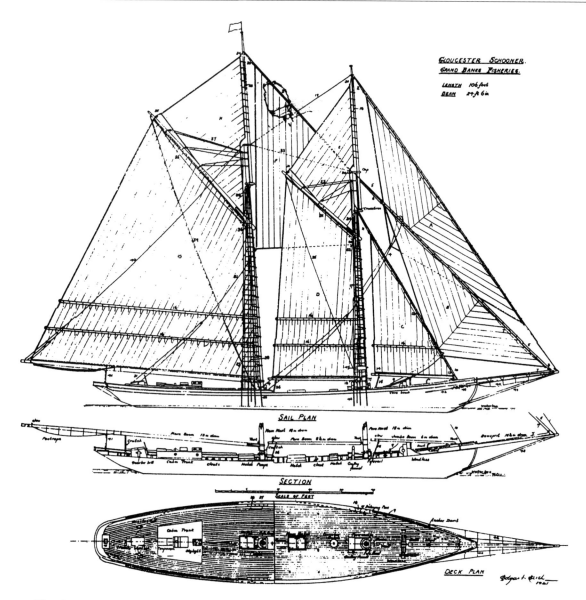

General arrangement plan, sail and rigging plan above the load waterline of a typical Gloucester Schooner for fishing on the Grand Banks, as drawn and reconstructed by Edgar J. March. Dimensions on plan: length 106ft, beam 24.5ft. (David MacGregor Plans)

The French employed three-masted barquentines and a few big schooners to fish on the Newfoundland Grand Banks and called them *terra neuvas*. The two-masted schooners which they sent to fish for cod off Iceland were called *morutiers* and they were large vessels carrying a crew of twenty-six men; in their hull-form they had considerable drag aft and they were really a modified version of a Gloucester fishing schooner. The cod was salted as soon as it was caught and to transport it back to market another type of schooner was employed. This was the *chasseur* which had a crew of five or six men and was designed to sail fast, resembling the *morutier* with a roller-reefing topsail but lacking the deep-heeled hull. These craft sailed down to Lisbon to load salt which they took up to Iceland to replenish the stock aboard the *morutiers*, taking in exchange the newly salted cod, which they then raced back to the French market.

Denmark possessed a few schooners fitted with wet wells to carry fish directly back home from the fishing fleet.

Above: Racing for the Fisherman's Cup in 1931, showing the Gertrude L Thebaud *(left) with an overall length of 134.5ft and the* Bluenose *(right) with her 81ft main boom. In this year, the latter won all three races. The pair again met in 1938 when* Bluenose *won three out of five races. The big four-sided 'fisherman's' staysail set from the main topmast was a typical feature of these schooners.* (Courtesy Nova Scotia Museum, Halifax)

Right: The Helen B Thomas *was the first 'knockabout' fishing schooner and was built in 1902 at Essex, Massachusetts, without a bowsprit, from a design by McManus.* (Courtesy of the Peabody Museum of Salem)

The clipper-bowed fishing schooner Unique *was built at Essex, Massachusetts, in 1887 with dimensions of 74.2ft x 22.2ft x 8.5ft and of 75 tons net. As she had no fore topmast she could only set a topsail on the mainmast. Schooners of her type were popular in the mackerel fishery and in spite of their sharp lines were given heavy quarters to carry the huge mainsails then popular. They were broad in proportion to their length and of shallow draft compared with the Grand Banks schooners. (Courtesy of the Peabody Museum of Salem)*

Above: The pinky Wave Queen *as photographed in 1911 beside a wharf at Digby, Nova Scotia, on the Bay of Fundy. The peculiarity of this craft was her 'pink' stern in which the planking was cocked-up and run astern to enclose the rudder head. Her rig consisted of two pole masts setting gaff sails and a single headsail on a bowsprit. They were used for inshore fishing up to the 1890s. The* Wave Queen *was built at St Andrews, NB, in 1879 with dimensions of 30.2ft x 11.7ft x 5.1ft. I am grateful to Dr Charles Armour for these particulars and for obtaining this print. (Frederick William Wallace Collection, Maritime Museum of the Atlantic, Halifax, NS)*

Below: The whaling schooner Elvira *was built at Misato, Japan, in 1898 and was registered in Alaska by 1911. Judging by the rigging, she undoubtedly had a topmast on each mast, but there are no braces to suggest yards, unless they led to blocks further up the lower mast head. (Courtesy of the National Maritime Museum, San Francisco)*

A large four-masted schooner loading supplies at St John's, Newfoundland, c1948, preparatory to sailing for the cod-fishing grounds on the Grand Banks. Built of wood this schooner, although heavily engined, still set gaff sails on each mast with topsails above and also four headsails. In 1950, the Portuguese had six four-masted schooners built of wood in the Grand Banks fleet, and the vessel pictured here was probably one of them. (Private collection)

17 | *School Ships*

THERE USED to be proper vessels for training boys to take up posts in sea-going merchantmen, and although a few schooners were employed, the majority of the vessels were square-rigged with three masts. In the chronologically-arranged list of vessels which Harold Underhill published in his *Sail Training and Cadet Ships* (1956), there were only four schooners used for training purposes in the years 1838-1914, out of ninety-seven vessels listed. There had been a number of brigs, a few brigantines and some barques, but they were mostly full-rigged ships; of the four schooners, two were British with auxiliary engines and rigged as three-masted topsail schooners, although one had been a naval gunboat; the other two were Danish and built of wood. From 1915-39 (inclusive), Underhill lists twenty-two schooners from various countries, including two with five masts. The first schooner designed specifically for training purposes was the *Juan Sebastian de Elcano* which the Spanish Government had built in 1927 as a four-masted auxiliary of 3220 tons displacement. Still afloat today, she sets gaff sails on each mast and crosses four yards on the foremast by which means she sets double topsails and a topgallant. Another surviving four-master is the *Almirante Saldanha*, built of steel for Brazil in 1933 and of much the same size. She has a very similar rig except that the fore gaff sail is

The Polish training schooner Iskra, *ex*-St Blane, *ex*-Vlissingen, *was built in 1917 in Holland and at first traded across the North Sea and English Channel until sold to Glasgow owners in 1925 who renamed her* St Blane. *Two years later she was sold to the Polish Government who ran her until the outbreak of the Second World War, when she was taken to Gibraltar for safety; she served as a supply ship and was returned to Poland after the War. I have not followed her subsequent career.* (Private collection)

In Torbay, August 1962, the day before the 'Tall Ships Race' began, one of the two French schooners – probably L'Etoile *– sailed by on the starboard tack. This schooner and her twin sister,* La Belle Poule, *were both built of steel in 1932 of 227 tons displacement. They are still sailed by the French Navy and are copies of the topsail schooners sailing out of Brittany in the 1930s.* (Courtesy of Patricia M A Purcell Gilpin)

replaced by staysails set from the mainmast which results in a sort of schooner-barquentine rig on the same basis as the schooner-brigantines described in Chapter 8.

More schooners were either built during the 1930s or commenced their duties in that decade: these included such well-known vessels as the steel French schooners *La Belle Poule* and *L'Etoile*, both built in 1932, and frequently to be seen with their white hulls and roller-reefing square topsails, which are reminiscent of the schooners from Brittany which used to visit British ports prior to the Second World War. Another vessel was the Belgian *Mercator*, also launched in 1932 and rigged initially as a three-masted topgallant yard schooner, but found to be over-canvassed and unstable, with the result that within twelve months she was converted to barquentine rig with shortened masts and the addition of more ballast. (See *Windjammer* 1993 No 4 published by Mariners International). Scandinavian countries liked sail-training vessels: Norway had three square-rigged vessels; Denmark had two, but also some schooners such as the two-master *Lilla Dan* built in 1951 and the three-master *Peder Most*, built during the War. Sweden also liked sail-training and produced the four-masted motor-sailer *Albatros* in 1942 with Bermudian sails on each mast, and five years later came the two-masted gaff-rigged sister ships *Falken* and *Gladan*, each with a spoon bow and fitted with a yard on the foremast to set a square sail. Another training vessel owned by Sweden from 1945-65 was the three-masted topsail schooner *Sunbeam II*, formerly Lord Runciman's yacht, which was renamed *Flying Clipper* in 1955.

In Great Britain, sail training had almost disappeared, with the *Prince Louis* of the Outward Bound Moray Sea School being probably the sole representative.

However, in 1955 after seventy-eight years of service, she was sold for breaking-up, but a replacement was found in the shape of the three-masted *Peder Most* of Svendborg which was renamed *Prince Louis II*. The University of Southampton School of Navigation did operate the auxiliary ketch *Moyana*, so that these two vessels, according to Underhill, were the only two sail training vessels under the British flag in 1955. A year later the first race of international sail-training ships was staged in Torbay, with a course from there to Lisbon, and the only schooner flying a British flag was the three-masted staysail schooner *Creole* which was loaned by a

The two-masted schooner Lilla Dan *under sail in Svendborg Sound in 1953. She was built two years earlier at Svendborg, Denmark, by J Ring Andersen for the Lauritzen Shipping Co and measured 120 tons with a length of 84.6ft. The owner's logo on the lower topsail is coloured red.* (Author)

Above: Under sail aboard the Lilla Dan *in 1953 with a freshening breeze. The upper topsail has been furled, and the two gaff sails have been reefed – the foresail by rolling it round the boom and the mainsail with reef points.* (Author)

Right: The Peder Most, *nearest to the camera, racing with the* Lilla Dan *(seen under her bowsprit) in Svendborg Sound in 1953. The latter has a square sail set from her fore yard and also a main gaff topsail. The* Peder Most *was built of wood in 1944 for A E Sørensen of Svendborg of 160 tons, and was at first named* Nette S. *In 1955 she was purchased by the Outward Bound Sea School at Burghead for about £11,500 and renamed* Prince Louis. *One of her masters in this capacity was Commander Graham de Chair RN, who told me that she once made 18 knots for two hours when running for shelter before a Force 8 gale. The School sold her in 1968 to a French organisation, Les Amis de Jeudi-Dimanche, who renamed her* Bel Espoir. (F Holm-Petersen Collection)

firm registered in Bermuda and manned by cadets from the Royal Naval College at Dartmouth. Other schooners which participated were the three-masted *Flying Clipper* and the *Bellatrix*, the latter being a yacht owned and skippered by the Portuguese Ambassador in London. But ten years were to elapse before the Sail Training Association, which was responsible for this event, launched its first schooner, the *Sir Winston Churchill*, followed two years later by a very similar three-master, the *Malcolm Miller*.

The *Sir Winston Churchill* was built at Hull by Richard Dunston Ltd and has a length of 150ft overall, a maximum beam of 25ft and a gross tonnage of 219; height of the mainmast above the deck is 97ft 9in and the total sail area is 7110 sq ft. Her twin 135hp diesel engines give a speed of 9.5 knots. She was due to be launched on 9 November 1965 by Princess Alexandra, but at the end of October an accident occurred on a wet windy day during which the vessel slid a few feet down the slipway and fell over on to her starboard side, snapping the newly-stepped masts. This delayed the launch until 7 February 1966 when she entered the water without any ceremony. Her sister-ship, the *Malcolm Miller*, was launched two years later; she has the same length but is 1ft 8in broader which increases her tonnage. Both vessels set gaff sails on fore and main with jib-headed topsails above; the mizen is a Bermudian sail; on the fore topmast there are two yards to set a square topsail, a raffee to the masthead and a squaresail from the lower yard; there are four headsails. Each schooner usually carries a permanent crew of six and about forty boys or girls. In a message to the Sail Training Association, its Patron, Prince Philip, wrote: 'This is a scheme designed to benefit the young men of this country, to give them a taste of fright, discomfort and adventure in an age when it is possible to live comfortably, securely and boringly'.

Boys, or girls for that matter, were only rarely now being trained under sail and the emphasis became more one of adventure and improvement of seamanship, and this has resulted in many vessels being fitted out, a few specially built and others converted from such diverse hulls as trawlers or lightships. The international races of these vessels, now rejoicing in the soubriquet of 'Tall Ships'–presumably borrowed from John Masefield's poem *Sea Fever*, when a tall ship was a queenly square-rigger–were at first scheduled to occur at two-year intervals, but rapidly became annual events. At a recent count, Rick Hogben said there were no less than thirteen brigs afloat, so the number of schooners must be considerable. Some of them are modern versions of the rig and others are replicas from the last century and, although sailing in ballast, their appearance has prompted nostalgic memories amongst landlubbers and drawn some cryptic comments from old sailors.

A fine sight in Falmouth Bay on 9 July 1966 as one of the Swedish schooners – probably the Falken *– sails by in a light breeze, with the other Swedish schooner, the* Gladan, *not far astern. They each carry a yard on the foremast to set a square sail in a fair wind.* (Author)

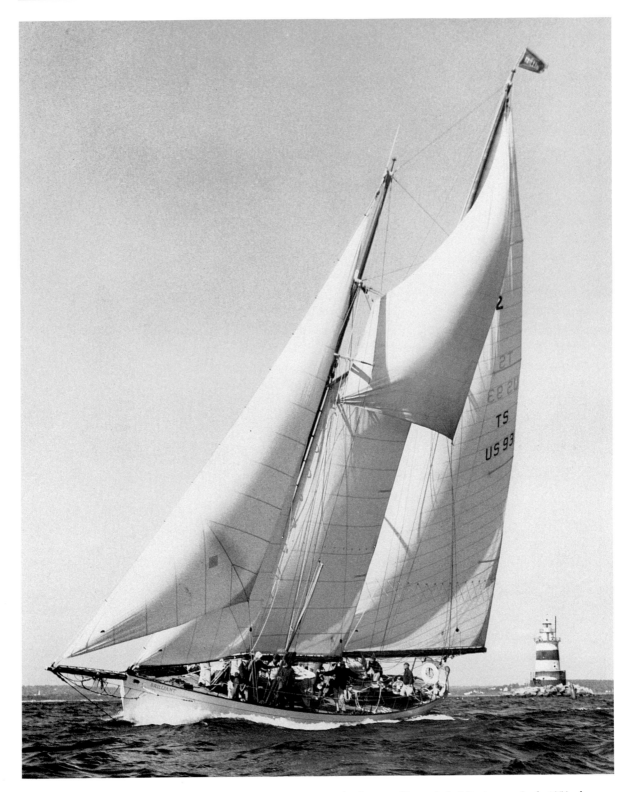

Built in 1932 as a gaff-rigged yacht, the Brilliant *won the east-bound transatlantic race to Plymouth the following year. In the 1950s she was given a tall Bermudian mainsail but retained her gaff foresail; in 1962 Captain 'Biff' Bowker took charge of her. By the end of the 1970s she was making eighteen trips per year for the Mystic Seaport training project for teenagers. This photograph shows the 61ft schooner leaving Latimer's Light astern in October 1977. (M A Stetts Photo, Mystic Seaport, Connecticut)*

Below: In a light breeze off Great Yarmouth in 1979, the Malcolm Miller *has her square topsail and raffee set but there is not enough wind to make her heel over. She is owned by the Sail Training Association of Great Britain and was built of steel at Aberdeen in 1968 of 219 tons gross, an overall length of 150ft and a maximum beam of 25ft; height of the mainmast above the deck is 97ft 9in. She has a permanent crew of six and can carry forty boys or girls. Her sister ship,* Sir Winston Churchill, *was built two years earlier with the same length but is 1ft 8in narrower.* (Author)

Above: The British three-masted Malcolm Miller *on a broad reach with all her fore-and-aft canvas set but her square sails furled.* (George A Osbon)

Left: To replace the schooner Prince Louis, *the Dulverton Trust built the three-masted topgallant yard schooner* Captain Scott *which was launched in 1970. She was built of larch on oak frames with steel deck beams in the yard of Herd & Mackenzie of Buckie; she had a length of 144ft 3in and a beam of 28ft 0in. Her rig was that of a typical ocean-going merchant schooner such as in the 'Western Ocean Yacht' category. She was sold in 1978 to interests in Oman for sail training at sea.* (Private collection)

18 | Schooners Today

BEFORE CONSIDERING the schooners that are either afloat today or that have been preserved for posterity, a word should be said about some old sailing ship hulls that were re-rigged as schooners during the Second World War. In 1941, the gambling barge *Rex*, ex-*Star of Scotland*, ex-*Kenilworth*, of 2308 tons gross which had been built of steel as a four-masted barque at Glasgow in 1887, lay abandoned in Los Angeles Harbour. In that year she was acquired by new owners, fitted out for ocean voyages and re-rigged as a six-masted schooner with 150ft Oregon pine masts setting Bermudian sails on each mast and also a yard on the foremast to set a square sail. Leaving in January 1942, she took a cargo of timber to Cape Town in 120 days and then in November the same year, bound to Brazil, she was sunk by shellfire from a German submarine. Another gambling barge, the *Tango*, also lying at Los Angeles, was refitted as a six-masted schooner in 1941; she was formerly the four-masted barque *Hans* built in 1904 at Hamburg and was re-named *Cidade do Porto* in 1943, and owned in Portugal. In 1942-43, the *Daylight*, built in 1902 at Port Glasgow as a four-masted barque of 3756 tons, was re-rigged as a six-masted schooner, but in 1944 her name changed to *Tangara* and her rig was now that of a four-masted barquentine owned in Brazil. (The information about the name and rig alterations is sketchy and may need verification.)

In Eastern Europe, Finland was constructing sailing vessels in the years 1945-52 to meet Russia's reparation demands in respect of the war between the two countries, and this was not a case of a few vessels but an immense fleet of no less than 105 schooners and barquentines. They were produced by four shipyards in a sort of mass production manner. They were three-masted and built of wood with auxiliary engines of 225hp; dimensions were 147.3ft length overall, 31.9ft beam, 11.3ft depth; tonnage varied between 320-330 tons gross and 190-210 tons net; sail area, according to rig, varied from 8825 to 9040 sq ft. Some of the schooners carried

The ungainly six-masted schooner rig given to the Cidade do Porto *in 1941 transformed the hull of the former four-masted barque* Mary Dollar, *ex-*Hans, *built in 1904. She is here seen at Lourenço Marques in 1945, deep-laden with coal. Trading under sail during the War, she earned some high freights; her last passage ended at Lisbon in 1946 and she was broken up two years later.* (Nautical Photo Agency)

Seen at Wiscasset, Maine, in 1964 and subsequently, are the disintegrating hulls of two four-masters: the Hesper *(left) and the* Luther Little, *which had arrived there in 1932 and had been waiting ever since then for cargoes to load. Sadly, by the first months of 1997, it was reported that the masts had fallen, the decks had collapsed and now the remains consisted of broken frames and fragments of these once fine schooners. (Author)*

standing topgallant yards. The engines gave them 7 knots and they could make the same speed under sail. Basil Greenhill, who provided me with this information, saw one of them at Helsinki in 1984 and another in the Black Sea a year later, and now reports that of this huge forgotten fleet only one remains. She is the *Vega*, said to be a handsome barquentine and is now being re-built at Pietarsaari in Finland for use as a sail training vessel. The construction of a huge fleet of wooden schooners and barquentines and their equally quick demise is reminiscent of the numbers built in North America in the years 1917-20.

The existence and movements of some of the surviving commercial schooners

The three-masted motor schooner Fyris *with pole masts and bowsprit. This is possibly the vessel built at Stade, River Elbe, Germany, in 1940. By 1973 she was Danish with a gross tonnage of 290. (George A Osbon)*

Above: Many hulks of old sailing vessels have been broken up since the end of the Second World War, and Basil Greenhill (on extreme left) and I watched this man smashing up the timbers of the old ketch Effort *at Galmpton, on the River Dart, in June 1952. He had bought the remains for £1.50. The* Effort *of 31 tons was built at Kingsbridge in 1880.* (Author)

Below: The bow carving on the three-masted schooner Kathleen & May, *photographed at Appledore quay in May 1954. She had been built in 1900 as the* Lizzie May *in the yard of Ferguson & Baird at Connah's Quay in North Wales and is reputed to have cost £2700. After many years of trade, followed by neglect from lack of funds, she was saved by the Maritime Trust and opened to the public in 1971 at Plymouth. She was later placed on exhibition in London, and in 1996 was sold to the Tall Ships Restoration Trust. She is now in Gloucester awaiting restoration.* (Author)

Left: Seen in the River Thames in August 1975 from the deck of the Charlotte Rhodes *were the two-masted Polish schooner* Zew Morsa *(ahead) and the three-masted topsail schooner* Bel Espoir, *ex-*Prince Louis, *ex-*Peder Most, *ex-*Nette S. (Author)

Below: Aboard the three-masted topsail schooner Charlotte Rhodes *in August 1975, under sail in the River Thames, and looking forward with the mainsail in the foreground.* (Author)

were recorded in the columns of *Log Chips* in July 1954 (Vol III). The auxiliary schooner *Adventure* (1926), last dory trawler out of New England, was to become a dude schooner out of Rockland, Maine; the auxiliary schooner *Bowdoin* left Boothbay Harbour for Labrador in June on her owner-master's 30th Arctic voyage; the three-masted schooner *Charles R Wilson* was bought by Ernie Mahood and beached near his logging camp at Stillwater in British Columbia; the three-master *Hispaniola*, ex-*Ryelands* (1877) after use in the filming of 'Treasure Island' had been sold to the town of Scarborough as a tourist attraction, and was then re-sold for the filming of 'Moby Dick'; the *Juan Sebastian de Elcano* was on a training cruise, already nine months old, between ports in the South and North Atlantic; the three-masted schooner *Vema* arrived New York on 4 June from a geophysical exploration cruise in the Caribbean and Gulf of Texas which began on 8 January; and the three-masted dude schooner *Victory Chimes*, ex-*Edwin & Maud* was reported in distress off the Maine Coast, but managed to reach Rockland to begin another cruise.

The above is just a sample of what some survivors were doing and the list can be continued to include other names. For example, the Australian three-

Above: At the start of a race in 1979 from Great Yarmouth for fore-and-aft rigged vessels, they are drifting in the North Sea for lack of wind. In the foreground is the Dutch schooner Eendracht, *fitted with blue sails on a blue hull.* (Author)

Right: The Aar, *ex-*Patricia A, *built in 1932, seen discharging at Teignmouth in 1960. About 1980 it was reported that she was being converted to carry more canvas.* (MacGregor Collection)

masted schooner *Alma Doepel*, built in 1903 in New South Wales for inter-colonial trade, as it was called then, was still afloat in 1970 as a motor ship trading out of Hobart. Eight years later she was acquired by Sail & Adventure Ltd to be refitted, and perhaps the name of this organisation epitomises what many feel is the attraction to be found in schooners today. The three-masted topsail schooner *Aquila Marina*, built in Denmark in 1920, has been saved from becoming a floating restaurant in Florida and was sailing in the Mediterranean in 1982. The motorised cargo-carrying schooner *Aar* of 204 tons gross, built of steel in Germany in 1932, was trading until the late 1960s; by 1979 she had been acquired by other parties, renamed *Patricia A*, and was being refitted at Newcastle for trade in the West Indies, where economies in the use of fuel were expected to be made with a larger sail area. This area is now thronged with schooners of every description but tight cruising schedules insist that engine power is regularly brought into use.

The use of newly-built schooners to carry cargo again is shared by a few enthusiasts who were responsible for the construction of the two-masted centreboard schooner *John F Leavitt* at Thomaston, Maine, in 1979. On a passage to Haiti with a cargo of timber, she was unfortunately abandoned on 28 December 1979 off Cape May, Delaware Bay, in bad weather with the vessel making water, and although she was not actually seen to sink no derelict has been found. No auxiliary engine had been installed.

Schooner yachts have always been popular in the United States, both large and small, and the gaff rig has remained in favour. Some replicas have latterly been constructed such as the topsail schooner *Shenandoah* in 1964, based on the Customs cutter *Joe Lane* of 1849. A replica of the famous *America* was produced in 1967 at a cost of $500,000 which was twenty-five times greater than the cost of the original. Several ports in Maine have fleets of two and three-masted schooners used for adventure and holiday cruises, and an example is provided by the *Heritage* operating out of Rockland. Her base is a few hundred yards from where the clipper ship *Red Jacket* was launched in 1853. This two-masted schooner is owned by Captains Douglas and Linda Lee who are also joint masters; she was first launched in April 1983 and measures 94.5ft in length, 24ft beam and has a draft of 8ft, but with the centreboard lowered the draft is extended to 18ft. The *Heritage* carries gaff sails on each mast, a jib-headed topsail on the mainmast but not one on the fore; however, there is a fore topmast to enable a flying jib to be hoisted high up on the stay which leads from the topmast head to the outer end of the jibboom. This gives her three headsails and makes a very pretty sight.

To determine the number of schooners still in use, or that are preserved in some form whether afloat, in dry dock or ashore, a study of Norman Brouwer's work, *Historic Ships*, is recommended. First published in 1985, it is now in its second edition.

There is mounting enthusiasm today for the re-establishment of the smaller classical rigs from the days of commercial sail – brig, brigantine, barquentine, schooner, ketch and cutter – and with gaff sails rather than Bermudian. On the opening page of his now classic book, *Wake of the Coasters*, the late John Leavitt wrote in 1970 that 'the dude cruisers are only maritime ghosts in an atomic world' and yet it looks as if their apparitions will increase both to haunt and to entertain us in the future.

Right: Built in 1977, the Pride of Baltimore *is a faithful reproduction of the Baltimore clipper type, and is owned and operated by the city of Baltimore. The fore topgallant has been sent down and the main topsail is not set. She is steered with a tiller.* (Author)

Below: The schooner Heritage, *operating from Rockland, Maine, was built in 1983 and is employed for adventure and pleasure cruises in company with other similar vessels. She has a permanent crew of nine and berths for thirty-three guests. Her main lower mast is 81ft from deck to cap, the main topmast is 34ft overall and the doubling is 8ft; the length of the main boom is 55ft. Some of the other schooners sailing out of Rockland and neighbouring ports have only pole masts or shorter topmasts, so the* Heritage's *tall topmasts make her a queen.* (Collection of Douglas K & Linda J Lee)

Short Reading List

Charles A Armour and Thomas Lackey, *Sailing Ships of the Maritimes* (Toronto 1975)

William A Baker,
Colonial Vessels (Barre, Mass. 1962)
Sloops & Shallops (Barre, Mass. 1966)

Norman J Brouwer, *International Register of Historic Ships* (Oswestry 1985)

Robert Carse, *The Twilight of Sailing Ships* (London 1965)

Howard I Chapelle,
The Baltimore Clipper (Salem, Mass. 1930)
The History of American Sailing Ships (New York 1935)
American Sailing Craft (New York 1936)
The Search for Speed under Sail 1700-1855 (New York 1967)

Arthur H Clark, *The History of Yachting* (New York 1904)

B B Crowninshield, *Fore-and-Afters* (Boston Mass. 1940)

Basil Greenhill,
The Merchant Schooners (2 vols, London 1951 and 1957; revised Newton Abbott 1968; 1 vol revised London 1988)
Schooners (London 1980)

Basil Greenhill and Sam Manning, *The Schooner 'Bertha L Downs'* (London 1995)

Henry Hall, *Report on the Ship-Building Industry of the United States* (New York 1970 reprint of original 1884 ed)

Peter Heaton, *Yachting: a History* (London 1955)

Frode Holm-Petersen,
Skibe og Søfolk fra Svendborgsund (Denmark 1963)
Maritime minder fra Marstal og Ærøskøbing (Denmark 1979)

Garry J Kerr, *Australian and New Zealand Sail Traders* (Blackwood, South Australia 1974)

John Leather, *Gaff Rig* (London 1970)

John F Leavitt, *Wake of the Coasters* (Mystic, Conn. 1970)

John Lyman (compiler and editor), *Log Chips* (4 vols Washington 1948-1959)

David R MacGregor,
Fast Sailing Ships 1775-1875 (Lymington 1973, revised ed London 1988)
Merchant Sailing Ships 1775-1815 (2nd ed London 1985)
Merchant Sailing Ships 1815-1850 (London 1984)
Merchant Sailing Ships 1850-1875 (London 1984)

E P Morris, *The Fore-and-Aft Rig in America* (New Haven, Conn. 1927)

Paul C Morris, *Four-Masted Schooners of the East Coast* (Orleans, Mass. 1975)

John P Parker, *Sails of the Maritimes* (Halifax, N.S. 1960)

W J Lewis Parker, *The Great Coal Schooners of New England 1870-1909* (Mystic, Conn. 1948)

Robert Simper, *Sail: the Surviving Tradition* (London 1979)

H Warrington Smyth, *Mast and Sail in Europe and Asia* (2nd ed Edinburgh and London 1929)

Harold A Underhill, *Sail Training and Cadet Ships* (Glasgow 1956)

Index